Created and designed by the editorial
staff of Ortho Books

Written and edited by
Janeth Johnson Nix

Photographed by
Clyde Childress

Special Consultant
Peggy Brandstrom Pavel

Front and back
cover photography by
Fred Lyon

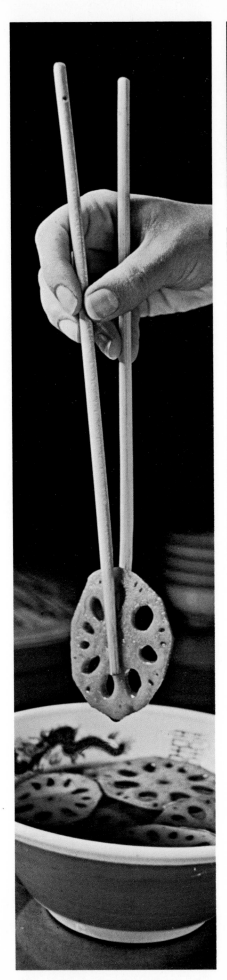

Adventures in Oriental Cooking

Contents

What this book is all about

Oriental cooking is an adventure that can be experienced in any kitchen. The author's combined knowledge and experience in Oriental cooking techniques and American home economics have been blended here to meet the needs of the American cook.

In order to tell you what this book is all about, I must spend a bit of time talking about myself. I am a California home economist and food writer with an insatiable appetite for, and boundless interest in, Oriental cooking in general and Oriental vegetables in particular.

Almost all of my life I've been surrounded by Orientals as friends, and for at least twenty years I've made very special demands upon them: "Tell me what it is. Show me how you do it." Most of these friends are Japanese, Chinese, or Korean; some are nationals, some are second or third generation; all have been heroically obliging. You will meet many of them in this book, and a few of them in this chapter.

Far East visit

In 1967 my husband and I made an extensive trip to the Orient. We had spent years getting ready for it. Ken studied Japanese, and we both soaked up every detail we could about history, culture, and habits—their whole way of life. We spent at least six months in detailed planning. This involved consulting our friends for itineraries, suggestions, food adventures (what restaurants to go to, food dishes to order), and local introductions.

The introductions proved to be excess baggage because many old friends had returned to the Far East. We had shown them, way back then, *our* country; they were determined

◁
You can feel like an adventuresome tourist even at home when you spend a day shopping in Oriental markets.

now, to show us *theirs.* And show us they did—shrines, gardens, amusements, homes, kitchens—all from the inside out. They told us the same thing we had told them: that curious, exhilarated strangers can absorb more about a country in a few weeks than citizens might in a lifetime.

I kept a diary of that trip, thinking it was a traveler's journal. It wasn't. It was a cook's tour, complete with descriptions, drawings, names, serving notes, and tentative analyses of everything we ate in Hong Kong, Taiwan, Korea, and Japan. Even floor plans. You will find many of these notes throughout the book.

Move to Japan

Then, much to our surprise and delight, Ken's company transferred us to Japan less than two years later. We would be in Kobe for three years and I resolved to spend those years indulging my curiosity and appetite. My

Shopping is the same the world over. It's looking for the freshest and best.

first decision was not to have a maid, though I eventually hired Megumi, a college girl, to come in once a week to help me translate. For the first six months we had a stove with an oven that had no temperature control and no broiler, so I plunged into top-of-the-stove Oriental cooking with enthusiasm. I had studied Chinese cooking and had learned much from our Japanese friends, but even so, much of my early cooking was a matter of experimentation. I would go to shops, buy what looked interesting, bring it home, and then figure out what to do with it. We had some exotic concoctions, needless to say. You will find few of these here, although my patient family put up with them all.

Exchange cooking lessons

Eventually, I started to give lessons in American cooking to Japanese women. More friendships developed, and I was able to make the same requests from them as I did from

In Japan, the author's morning purchases are tied and carried in furoshiki *(scarf).*

If you can't find Oriental vegetables in the market, you can grow your own. These gardens in Locke, California supply the entire community. Oriental vegetable seeds are becoming easier for the home gardener to find too.

friends at home: "Show me how. Tell me more." One of my most rewarding memories is of the seven hours I spent cooking with a friend and her 84-year-old mother. We ate for two hours after cooking this great feast, and I felt I had a thorough grounding in several traditional techniques as well as modern practices. You will find some of the recipes and all of the techniques and practices in this book.

It interested me to discover, both in Japan and America, that Oriental cooking practices change as they pass from generation to generation. But why should that be a surprise? Many of our dishes, too—like grandmother's mince pie, or mother's fresh bread—are more a matter of nostalgia than actuality.

Theories and methods

This book is not a dictionary of Oriental cookery, nor is it a compre-hensive rundown on Far Eastern cuisine. It is only one cook's approach to some of the adventures and pleasures and secrets of Oriental cookery. And because I have three meals a day that I must get on the table, it is Oriental cookery family-style, tailored to an American kitchen and American stores and American schedules and American eating patterns.

Nor is this only a recipe book, although I have included many. Rather, it is a book about theories and methods—a lowdown on what many Oriental cooks take for granted because they've learned to cook as we did—through imitation of mothers, not through following recipes. Just as Western cooking is mostly a matter of absorbing a few basic principles and methods and adapting them to various ingredients and situations, so is Oriental. I've tried to ferret out as many of their basic techniques as possible and present them throughout the book:

how to keep vegetables crisp, how to cook rice and noodles, how to make stocks, and, of course, how to put it all together into a company dinner, a family supper, a picnic, whatever.

Grow my own

I am fortunate to live in an area where I have access to many unusual Oriental vegetables both from markets and gardens of my friends. But as my family's interest and consumption of these vegetables increased along with the availability of seeds, I wanted to have my own supply. Since some Oriental vegetables are grown only in limited quantities for specialized markets, they are expensive to buy, but not to grow, so it makes sense to plant your own. Happily they require no more care than corn or string beans. The chapter on vegetable growing (page 80) is filled with gardening specifics.

Because so much of Oriental cook-

Bulging crates of bok choy are sent to U.S. markets on a year-round basis.

In Locke, bok choy is in continuous supply because much of it is dried.

When a crab snaps back at you, you know it is fresh enough to buy.

ing is vegetable cooking, this is almost a vegetable book. I've included directions for cutting them (an art in itself), cooking them, saucing them, and arranging them as well as for growing.

Shopping and chopping

Many people think that Oriental cooking depends upon mysterious ingredients or strange equipment. This is not necessarily true, but a few special ingredients and tools are needed and a lot of others are fun to use. I have included a section describing these items and, in some cases, give hints on how to substitute for them.

Sometimes I think that half the pleasure of Oriental cooking is shopping in Oriental markets. The minute I get loose in one—sniffing all those exotic odors, examining all those colorful labels, poking at all those strange new vegetables—I'm a tourist in my own country. Once, when I suddenly came to, I discovered that I was alone in the store, locked in. "How could it happen?" wondered the tiny woman who finally rescued me. "You're so *big*—why didn't they see you?" (I'm 5 foot 7, but was probably bent over snooping around a low shelf.)

In Japan, I did what the Japanese do. I shopped every day, buying only what I needed for the next meal, feeling nicely frugal when I asked for meat by the gram instead of the pound. When we first returned to the United States I tried to carry my Japanese habits into the supermarket. My one green pepper, one turnip, and two carrots on the conveyor belt struck me as both pitiful and admirable as I watched the other customers with their bulging bags.

But it didn't last. I've reverted to bulging bags. The supermarkets, in fact, are surprisingly good hunting grounds, even when I'm focusing on Oriental cookery. As long as they continue every year to increase their stock of fresh vegetables, frozen wrappers, dried noodles, and bottled sauces and seasonings, who am I to resist?

Adventures in eating out

You might think that because we get so much Oriental food at home, my family would head straight to a steak house or a pizza parlor when we eat out. Not true. It's still a treat to go to Oriental restaurants, especially for me. That's when I sit back and luxuriate in service and new tastes without having to worry about getting everything and everyone to the table at once.

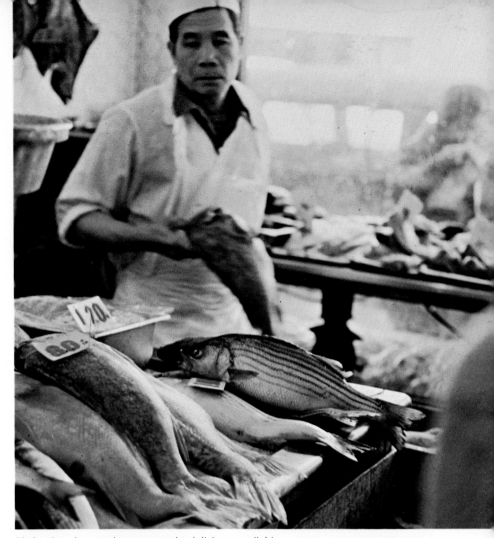

It's hard to choose when so many fresh fish are available.

One thing we never do in a Chinese restaurant is order a plate special, Dinner 1, 2, or 3 with a variety of things included. Not because these are not good foods, and not because in some restaurants these dishes are modified to suit American tastes (chop suey is more American than Chinese), but because these menus run very much to formula, and we like to keep trying new things.

Some foods, though, I order often: all the *dim sum,* and mandarin duck, and twice-cooked pork—anything that demands ticklish timing or last-minute attention. I can cook these things at home, but at home I cook them one at a time. To relax and have several things served at the peak of their perfection, is to me, very close to bliss.

In a Japanese restaurant I often order *tempura,* for the simple reason that at home I eat it last, and sometimes least. We all consider a traditional Japanese restaurant dinner an event. For everyone, it's partially nostalgia; for me it's the additional glory of enjoying all those courses served in beautiful dishes.

Not only do I enjoy trying new foods in restaurants, but I also get new menu ideas, especially in the small, busy ones where tables are shared or close together, or at convivial counters or *sushi* bars. Once past some occasional resistance on "what Americans would like," friendly customers and helpful waiters enjoy talking about food, and continue to come up with all kinds of ideas that are new to me.

Let me introduce you to . . .

Dozens of people have given me help on this book, some of them long before I knew there would be a book. First there were our friends, and the friends and relatives of friends; then there were the seed importers, horticulturists, vegetable wholesale people, and gardeners who helped on vegetable research. Some of them deserve special recognition because they have actually acted as consultants every step of the way: Ellen Fujioka, a *nisei* friend of long standing; Hannah Sato, who spent her teenage years in Japan; Jeannette Dare, a Chinese friend who grew up in San Francisco and showed me how to shop Chinatown.

Joe Ishizaki of Yamato's Restaurant in San Francisco has been a great help, as has Lawrence Chu of Chef

The author asks another question about Japanese cooking techniques—how to roll stuffed cabbage in a sudare.

Lawrence Chu. *It is important not to overcook vegetables in stir-frying.*

Jeannette Dare. *In any cooking, the final taste is what counts.*

Ellen Fujioka. *Fanning rice brings out its luster when you make* sushi.

Joe Ishizaki. Sashimi *is one of the better known Japanese specialties.*

Hannah Sato. *Low tide may reveal limpets or other shellfish for eating.*

Chu's Restaurant in Los Altos, California.

To say nothing at all of the communicative waiters and diners in restaurants, and nothing at all of the many clerks and customers I have corralled in markets, asking them just exactly what they were going to do with that particular vegetable, or that particular box. I remember with special fondness the two customers in San Francisco Chinatown who entered into a discussion of the merits of bitter melon, which had just come into season. "The bitter the better" was the consensus.

And to say nothing of my husband, Ken, and three sons who have served as a full-time taste panel, unsung, creative, and beautifully outspoken.

About those Oriental words

Although most of the ingredients and names for recipes in this book are familiar, you may come across some words which sound completely foreign. In many places I have used the Japanese or Chinese name because that is the way I first learned to identify something, or because that name is easiest to use when you are looking for it in an Oriental market.

A glossary of terms appears on pages 30-31. I hope you will use it as a guide when you go shopping. You'll be proud of yourself when you knowingly ask for *daikon* or *gow choy*, instead of radishes and chives.

Happy adventuring

You will find some traditional recipes in this book, but only a few. Most of these recipes have been tampered with, one way or another—by upcoming generations or other cultures, through expedience or through experimentation.

Nor will you find any real attempt to compare Chinese to Japanese to Korean. There are many, many differences, some obvious and some subtle, and the discovery of each is an adventure in itself—more rewarding, I feel, if it's a personal realization, rather than a textbook definition. More important, the differences do not pertain to this book; they have little to do with how a particular dish is going to work on an American table.

Because that's what *my* adventuring in Oriental food is all about: tonight's dinner for the family. Once in a while I prepare a traditional Japanese or Chinese or Korean dinner for guests, but that has been the least of the pleasures. The bigger reward is in counting on Oriental dishes regularly for variety in family meals. When I pull out all the stops and prepare traditional recipes to be served in the traditional way, the observance of letter-perfect ritual is important; it's a pleasure, but it's a production. When I consider the evening schedule—one son late because of baseball, another one leaving early because of work—and prepare Oriental food family-style, the method, our food preferences, and the contents of the refrigerator are all that matter.

So I cross cultures freely; I substitute with abandon; I ad lib with whatever is in season and on hand. But I take all liberties with deep gratitude to the traditionalists who have preserved and passed on their methods so that Oriental cookery is a current and adventurous way of life in my California kitchen.

I hope it will be in yours, too.

Fact and fiction about nutrition

It's impossible to delve very far into the subject of Oriental cooking without wondering about the nutritional value of the food. In passing on some questions I have been asked, I might also set some myths to rest.

"Does stir-fry cooking preserve more nutrients in vegetables than other methods of preparation?"

Yes, it preserves nutrients as well as color, flavor, and texture by reducing the amount of surface area exposed as well as reducing the amount of cooking liquid used and the length of cooking time. The water soluble vitamins are retained in the light sauce.

"Why do I feel hungry an hour after I eat Chinese food?"

There are lots of theories about this. A nutritionist might talk about the "burning-up" rates of the different foods. A dietitian might put it in terms of the satiety value of rice vs. bread, vegetable gravy vs. cream sauce, fresh fruit vs. a piece of apple pie. A restaurateur might tell you that you have simply composed your dinner poorly—that you didn't select the correct variety of dishes.

My guess is that there are some other reasons, too: 1. Americans just don't eat as much rice as the Orientals do. To Orientals, rice is the essence of the meal. To Americans, rice is nothing but high-calorie starch, something to be resisted. 2. Many Americans unconsciously save space for a dessert, and Chinese restaurants rarely provide more than a fortune cookie. 3. Milk with a meal and coffee afterwards seem more filling than tea throughout.

"Won't I gain weight on it? All those noodles and rice?" or "Isn't it by its very nature a reducing diet? All those vegetables?"

It's the same old story in the Orient as it is anywhere else: the amount of food you take in as well as the type of food you eat has a direct bearing on gaining or losing weight. The cook or the eater can stack the calorie deck either way.

Personally, I feel that it is easier to lose weight on Oriental foods than on American ones, mainly because I find a stir-fried dish with a bit of rice a complete and satisfying meal. Nor do I feel hungry afterwards, because many vegetables—particularly the leafy ones—contain so few calories that dietitians class them as "free" calories (foods that are high in nutrients but low in calories), I feel I can be good to myself and eat my fill.

"What about the fat level? I've heard that Orientals don't have any cholesterol problems, but what about all that cooking oil?"

Certainly stir-fried vegetables have a higher fat level than boiled or steamed vegetables—but so does a tossed salad have a higher fat level than a cold, marinated vegetable. In most of these recipes I have called for less oil than is usually used in restaurants, but I use the oil I *do* use with a clear conscience, having long ago made the bargain with myself that I willingly sacrifice the pat of melting butter on hot vegetables for the sake of enjoying every drop of the liquid-gravy.

It does appear to be true that Orientals have fewer cholesterol problems. Some say that it's because they use vegetable oils—others attribute it to their low consumption of dairy products and meat.

"How about protein? I rely on meat and dairy products to get the minimum daily requirements. How do they do it?"

It's easy for Americans to forget about fish as a source of protein, but it's a staple in Oriental diets. They use it all around the menu—not only fresh but canned, dried, salted; not only in serving-size quantities but as garnishes for soups, noodles, rice; not only straight but as a base for soups, sauces, seasonings.

They also rely on soybean, one of the world's two complete plant proteins. (The other one is wheat.) Sometimes called "the cow of the Orient," it shows up at almost every meal in one form or another: sprouts, cooking oil, soy sauce, *tofu* (curd), and *miso* (fermented paste).

In short, Orientals get much of their protein little by little (bonito flake by bonito flake, so to speak) instead of steak by steak, and they get many of their minerals and vitamins by preserving them within the vegetables or in the cooking gravy instead of throwing them away in their cooking water.

Putting it all together

If you've been wary of Oriental cooking, just think of it as something for everyday fare—the same as it is to Orientals. As you prepare the food, you'll find that it hasn't the mystique you thought it did. It's just something good to eat and a creative challenge you'll enjoy.

Many Chinese restaurants make a distinction between "family menus" and "banquet menus." Family style means that they serve all the food at one time; banquet style means that they serve as many as 10 courses in succession. Rice and tea might appear throughout, but there is no true main course.

Cooking at home

At home in my kitchen, when I'm preparing just Oriental food, I make distinctions too, but not quite the same ones. My categories are "family suppers" and "guest dinners."

Family suppers mean serving one dish along with rice (see page 61 for more on this). Guest dinners mean an evening of good conversation and unusual food: hors d'oeuvres, several dishes, plus a dessert and California wine.

At first when I planned an Oriental meal for guests, I puzzled how to put it all together. It was simple enough to follow a recipe but what should I serve it with? After or before? On? I decided that if the food is good, the combination doesn't matter, and I feel comfortable serving *teriyaki* with a green salad or fried rice with fried chicken.

Sometime, though, I hope you will enjoy, as I do, the challenge of serving an all-Chinese or all-Japanese dinner. But if Oriental cooking is new to you, don't get in over your head. Approach it slowly and practice first with individual recipes so it will continue to be a pleasure.

◊

A Chinese meal features a variety of small dishes rather than one main course.

Variety—spice of life

Considering Oriental food daily fare does not necessarily mean eating it every day. It's not the answer to every meal, every menu, any more than Mexican food would be. But opening your mind and your kitchen to *any* culture brings untold variety to daily menus. Here are some of my best discoveries for round-the-year, round-the-clock adventures in Oriental eating.

✓ *Bok choy* soup (see page 35) is hearty enough for a soup supper, or a soup-and-sandwich supper, or, with Chinese cabbage salad (page 41), a soup-and-salad supper.

✓ Raw Chinese cabbage or parboiled edible podded peas are a delicious addition to a green salad, whatever the dressing. So are mandarin orange sections, or raw bean sprouts. So is a sprinkling of sesame seeds.

✓ If you make your own salad dressing, try substituting one third of the oil with sesame oil, and add a small pinch of monosodium glutamate and a large one of sugar. The difference will surprise you.

✓ When a gang of teenagers needs filling up, try *udon* or *soba* in broth (page 47); or cellophane noodles with bits of meat and vegetables (page 49). (I've yet to meet a youngster who doesn't love noodles.)

✓ Stir-fried zucchini or green beans or any garden-fresh vegetable are perfect partners to barbecued meat, baked salmon, broiled chuck—any meat that forms no gravy of its own. The juices from the vegetables make up for the lack of meat gravy, with fewer calories and fresher flavor.

✓ Some mothers fill their kitchens with the aroma of cinnamon and baking cookies. I like to fill mine with the aroma of fried *won ton* (see page 36). When my youngest comes home from school with friends, *won ton* makes a great snack.

✓ *Sashimi* (see page 77) is an impressive first course for any dinner, Japanese or American.

✓ A jug of *miso* soup (see page 34) is as welcome as a jug of hot chocolate at tailgate dinners or cold-weather picnics or on all-day drives.

✓ For Boy Scout outings or neighborhood potlucks—wherever I suspect that casseroles will rule the day—I enjoy contributing chicken *teriyaki* (page 71) or *sushi* (page 50). One of the reasons they go so fast is that they're a surprise; no one expects to find Oriental food in a smorgasbord setting.

Menus, Chinese-style

Whether you cook it at home or order it in a restaurant, there's no mystery about a Chinese menu. Variety is what you're after: the contrast of sweet and sharp, bitter and bland, soft and crisp, subtle and strong. Even hot and cool—not temperatures but flavor. The Chinese, like the Indians, feel that "hot" foods (like bitter melon and curry) cool you off, and that "cool" foods (like rice and yogurt) warm you up.

Contrasting harmony

The Chinese call this contrast *Yin* and *Yang*. In philosophic terms, it's the balance of the elements (male and female, positive and negative, light and dark) for the sake of harmony. In menu terms, it's the contrast of flavors, textures, colors, for the sake of interest.

When we go to a restaurant, each member of the family selects one dish from each category of pork, poultry, beef, seafood, and vegetables. Sometimes there are too many duplicates: Too many are seasoned with ginger and oyster sauce, or contain the same combination of in-season vegetables, or are based on noodles. But the waiter helps us get a balance, and gives us other tips as well, such as that certain delicate dishes should be eaten before spicy ones. It takes time to order this way, but there's no better way to explore Chinese food than to consider the menu a sampler and to allow a helpful waiter to be a guide.

A numbers game

Because variety is the point, planning a Chinese menu is a numbers game. A meal for four calls for four dishes, plus rice, soup, and tea; a meal for six, six dishes . . . And so on.

At a restaurant this could easily mean "the more the merrier." At home, when I entertain, it's a different story.

For this reason I limit my Chinese dinner parties. Six people and six dishes are enough for me to cope with. In planning a Chinese dinner for guests, I do what I do with any guest meal: plan the menu around the cooking facilities, eliminating as much last-minute cooking as possible.

My master plan for a Chinese dinner party usually includes: 1) something from the top of the stove, usually a soup; 2) something from the oven (roast duck or roast pork); 3) something steamed (fish or spareribs); 4) a stir-fried dish; 5) something that can be done ahead and reheated (fried rice or dry braised prawns); and 6) something that can be done ahead because it was meant to be served cold (Chinese chicken salad). And I don't overlook the possibilities of buying things ready-made, such as all the *dim sum* savories, to make my menu planning and cooking easier.

Menus, Japanese-style

A traditional Japanese dinner is completely different from a Chinese one. The food is arranged ahead of time and served on individual dishes; at a very formal meal, six or eight dishes might be offered. Beauty is what counts. Food, table settings, atmosphere, view, all are carefully staged and synchronized.

When it comes to party-planning, I reduce a Japanese meal to these components: 1) something that can be prepared ahead—*suimono,* soup; 2) something to hold in the refrigerator (for last-minute assembly)—*sunomono,* salad; 3) a meat or poultry or fish for a main course; 4) a cold, dressed vegetable; 5) rice, pickles; and 6) tea, *sake,* or California wine.

Or I go the other way, as the Japanese often do, and serve a one-dish meal, like *sukiyaki* (page 66).

Oriental table settings

Setting the table for a guest meal is part of the fun. You don't really need a wide variety of dishes to set a good table. A bit of know-how and a bigger bit of imagination will serve you just as well.

For a Chinese meal, you need very little in the way of dishes. In homes each place setting consists of a rice bowl (it serves as a plate), a soup bowl, a soup spoon, a tea cup, and chopsticks. Restaurants provide a small plate as well because most Americans would rather have rice under or alongside other foods, and because plates are handy repositories for shells, bones, whatever.

When selecting a container for rice, any bowl you can hold in your hands will work—a dessert, cereal, or soup bowl—but a genuine rice bowl seems to make serving and eating the rice that much better.

For serving dishes, you need bowls, platters, or plates. The same platter that holds a turkey works fine for steamed fish, and a vegetable serving dish will serve as well for stir-fried zucchini as it will for mashed potatoes.

Japanese table settings are far more elaborate and studied compared to the Chinese, but take well to improvisation. One friend (exaggerating) claims that the Japanese use as many dishes for one place setting as the Chinese do for a whole meal. But because the Japanese don't believe in matched sets of dishes, you are operating within the spirit of tradition if you mix and match from your own cupboards.

Depending upon the menu, I use either a small bowl plus a small plate or a large dinner plate at each place. For the dipping sauces or condiments or "special bites" that they provide, you can make do with clam shells, nut cups, small ashtrays—or Japanese teacups. I often hunt bazaars and garage sales too, looking for unusual tableware.

Some of my favorite rummage-sale finds are pedestal English serving dishes, ironstone platters, and odd serving pieces that came from an incomplete set. One of my friends picked up some fan-shaped bowls that evidently came from a lazy-Susan chip-and-dip set, and another who likes folk art made her own slab pottery plates.

I always keep my eyes open for chopstick rests—small pieces of driftwood, fresh red peppers, shells, rocks—and I'm forever a pushover for baskets of any kind.

I use the baskets as serving dishes. For drippy foods, I line them with non-poisonous leaves from the garden: nandina, camellia, fig, strawberry. Sometimes I pass a basketful of steaming towels at the beginning (Japanese style) or end (Chinese style) of a meal.

Though it's hard for me to resist Oriental tableware, I feel no compulsion about confining table settings to it, even for traditional meals. As with the menus, authenticity is far less important than the spirit.

Party meals and special menus

Not all of my Oriental food ends up at parties. The following are some menus for a wide variety of occasions. Some are favorites of mine and some are favorites of Oriental friends.

Remember, as you assemble these recipes into menus of your own, that the serving estimates for recipes from the chapters themselves are for family meals, not for guest ones. Serving one dish plus rice on a busy evening is a very different thing from serving several dishes for guests on a convivial one.

As a rule of thumb: For guests, allow ⅓ pound meat, poultry, or seafood per person, plus vegetables, ½ cup rice, and luxuries. For family, allow 3 to 4 ounces meat, more vegetables, and all the rice they can eat. Go on the theory that family has access to the refrigerator, and that guests thrive on abundance.

The menus that follow are flexible; make substitutions, additions, or deletions as you will. If you choose, cook fewer dishes in larger quantities, or stagger their serving times. The adventure of Oriental cooking is not in cooking alone. It's in the creativity and confidence of the cook, and in the sharing of good food and good times with good friends.

A Chinese banquet at home

There is good reason why a formal Chinese banquet is usually a restaurant affair. Waiters appear with a continuous array of hot dishes, serve each as a separate course, and the number seems endless. You savor each item as it arrives and give silent thanks and praise to the cook at work in the kitchen.

I'm not one to be kitchen-bound when there are guests around, so I plan my banquets carefully, doing as much advance cooking as possible. I also put everything except the dessert on the table at the same time. The catch comes in doing just that.

It takes practice. I can't tell you just how long it takes; I know that I served a full Chinese meal to guests only after I was completely at ease with stir-frying. When it became automatic enough for me to cook and still think about last-minute details, I decided I could handle the dinner as well as enjoy the guests.

The dinner shown in the photo on page 8 is one that I serve often. Consider it a master plan. Vary the vegetable, vary the courses (I sometimes serve the prawns as hors d'oeuvres) and delete or expand or substitute as you wish. But precook as much as you can.

```
CHINESE BANQUET FOR 6
Golden Corn Soup
Dry Braised Prawns
Sweet and Sour Pineapple Pork
Spicy Steamed Fish
Velvet Chicken with Ham and Broccoli
Pea Pods with Mushrooms
Steamed Rice
Ginger Sundaes
Tea
```

Golden Corn Soup

This is a classic recipe, cooked in a modern way.

**1 can (1 lb. 1 oz.) cream-style corn
4 cups chicken stock or pork stock
　Salt
1 tablespoon cornstarch mixed with 2
　tablespoons water or stock
2 eggs
1 green onion and top, cut in 1-inch
　lengths and shredded, or 2 tablespoons
　shredded gow choy**

Whirl 1 cup of corn and 1 cup of stock in a blender. Combine with remaining corn and stock in a saucepan. Add salt to taste; heat slowly. Stir cornstarch-water mixture to recombine, add to soup, and cook until slightly thickened. Cool.

To serve, reheat. Beat eggs, add to soup; stir until cooked. Pour into

tureen and sprinkle with green onion. Serves 6.

Dry Braised Prawns

If you cook the prawns in the shell, you can cook them ahead of time. Follow the recipe on page 79, and remove from pan as soon as they are cooked. Place in a small baking pan and cover with foil. To reheat, bake in a hot oven (400°) for 10 minutes.

If you want dipping sauce, mix a little dry mustard with a few drops of water to make a smooth paste; blend in a drop of salad oil to make it shiny.

Put mustard on one side of the dipping bowls, and catsup on the other side.

Sweet and Sour Pineapple Pork

I cook this in my large electric frying pan before guests arrive.

Follow the recipe on page 63, making the following changes: Use 1½ pounds of pork cubes. Marinate meat, then dredge in flour before frying. Cook onion and green pepper only 1 minute before adding the pineapple. Immediately stop cooking. Cut 2 small tomatoes in wedges and place on top of the cooled meat.

At serving time, stir once, and cook just until heated through.

Spicy Steamed Fish

Prepare this early in the day, but cook it just before serving. A 2- to 2½- pound fish will serve six people at a Chinese meal.

Wash and scale whole fish, pat dry, and place on a plate or platter that will fit inside a steamer. (You can improvise a steamer in a roasting pan.) Mix together 1 tablespoon minced fermented black beans (rinse with water before mincing), 1 clove garlic, minced, 2 teaspoons minced ginger root, 1 tablespoon slivered chung choy (salted turnip), 2 tablespoons soy sauce, and 1 teaspoon each sugar, salt, and salad oil.

Rub mixture over and inside fish. Cut 2 green onions and tops in 1-inch lengths, shred, and sprinkle over fish. Cover with plastic film and refrigerate. To cook, steam for 20 minutes.

Velvet Chicken with Ham and Broccoli

Cook the chicken less than 3 hours before dinner so you won't need to refrigerate it. It should be served at room temperature; only the broccoli topping is hot.

Follow recipe for Velvet Chicken on page 71. Cool; remove meat from bones and cut in 1x2-inch strips.

Cut 8 sandwich-size slices of boiled ham in half; roll each slice. In a serving dish alternate strips of chicken and ham rolls. Set aside. Cook 1½ cups of broccoli flowerets in boiling salted water for 3 minutes; drain and rinse with cold water.

Heat 1 cup chicken stock (from cooking chicken) with 1 teaspoon each soy sauce and sherry. Taste, add salt if necessary. Mix 1 tablespoon each cornstarch and water; add to stock and cook until slightly thickened.

To assemble, reheat sauce, add broccoli, and let stand for 1 minute to heat through. Pour over chicken.

Pea Pods with Mushrooms

Slice vegetables, assemble seasonings, and mix gravy ingredients ahead of time. Cook at the last minute, following directions for basic stir-fried vegetables (page 55). Use ½ pound edible podded peas, ends and side strings removed, 10 whole dried mushrooms, presoaked, and ½ cup each sliced bamboo shoots, and sliced water chestnuts.

Cook peas; remove from pan. Cook mushrooms with bamboo shoots and water chestnuts; recombine with peas, and add gravy.

Steamed Rice

See recipe for Chinese-style rice on page 45. Figure on 1½ to 2 cups uncooked rice for 6 people.

Ginger Sundaes

If you want to satisfy a sweet tooth, try this. Stir 2 tablespoons chopped, candied or preserved ginger into ½ pint commercial sour cream. Let stand all day in the refrigerator so the ginger will soften. Serve as a topping over pineapple or orange sherbet.

Tea

Although most restaurants serve Oolong, there is no such thing as one particular kind of Chinese tea. They enjoy and serve many different kinds.

Generally the Chinese brew their tea on the subtle side—Americans may call this weak. It should have a pleasant natural sweetness, not a harsh bitter taste.

To brew tea, fill a teapot with boiling water. Pour water out and add from 2 to 4 heaping teaspoons of tea. Pour in 6 cups boiling water, cover, and let steep 3 minutes before serving.

You'll probably want to experiment with this and see what suits you—there is no right amount. Orientals brew several pots of tea from the same leaves, and some people think the flavor improves with each brewing.

You don't always find something to take home to eat, but the search is part of the fun at a beach picnic.

Sea snails are gathered for those who have the patience to cook and eat them.

In the right season, the tender leaves of some seaweed can be cut and dried.

Sliced *kamaboko*, hard boiled eggs, rice balls are fast to assemble for a picnic.

A converted army cot with a plywood top makes an ideal table for serving food.

Japanese picnic

To me, much of Japanese food seems to have been designed specifically for an outing: it is meant to be eaten at room temperature, it is easy to eat with fingers (or chopsticks), and it holds up well when prepared ahead of time. Japanese food may *look* as if it were intended for a banquet. The tradition of arranging food in a beautiful way holds whether the menu is as simple as rice balls, a bit of fish, and pickles, or is an elaborate six-course meal.

Adjustable menu

The picnic on these pages fed 12 people, but it could be adjusted downward by leaving out an item or two. It would also be easy to assemble a spur-of-the-moment picnic from the array of canned and prepared foods at a Japanese market.

If you're fortunate enough to have Japanese friends who will take you along when they go for clams, abalone, or mussels, you can count on learning some unusual ways to prepare them when you get home. They'll even turn you on to the food adventures of things you've never heard of—or, at least, things you have never considered eating. On one picnic I learned how to look for the right seaweed that was washed up on the beach after a winter storm; on another occasion we tracked down sea snails and limpets (for those who were patient enough to eat them); we've gone to the beach at night when the smelt were running and scooped the silvery fish from the sand after the men emptied their dip nets; we've hunted along the rocks in the bay for herring eggs laid on seaweed.

But any reason can be an excuse for a picnic at the beach and you should not pick up things if you don't know what you're doing. Check out local rules and regulations first. Some things are poisonous at certain times of the year, and many areas are protected or ecological reserves.

Picnic packing

In Japan, picnic food is often packed in lacquer boxes. For our outings, I use nice cans—the kind that rice crackers come in or that you buy cookies and fruit cake in at Christmas time—or covered plastic boxes. I stack the cans two or three deep in the middle of a *furoshiki* (see photo, page 3), a square of cotton material, and tie the opposite corners of the fabric to form a handle. A big *furoshiki* can also serve as a tablecloth.

Our family picnic table is an old card table with the legs sawn off to bring it nearer to the ground. Our friends, the Satos, use a converted army cot. The cot was cut down to one-half its size, using only two of the cross-legs, and a custom-cut sheet of plywood is bolted on, each time it is set up. The nuts and bolts are stored in a small drawstring bag which is tied to the cot frame.

Something new . . .

If you are new to Japanese foods, this menu might give you a faster introduction than you're ready for; it contains recipes you're not likely to run across in restaurants and vegetables that few supermarkets carry. But I figure that at a picnic it's sink or swim, so to speak, and I never worry about taking along unusual foods. The air and exercise not only stimulate appetites but can also open closed minds. At this particular picnic, children and adults alike licked their fingers and came back for seconds.

JAPANESE PICNIC FOR 12
Nishime   Glazed Smelt
Crisp Chicken Teriyaki
Rice Balls   Sushi
Hard-Boiled Eggs   Kamaboko
Pickles
Fresh Fruit
Soft Drinks   Beer

Nishime—Cooked Vegetables with Chicken

This dish contains a lot of vegetables that may be new to you. All are available in Japanese markets, but you can make substitutions, such as small potatoes in place of *taro,* and green beans in place of coltsfoot.

1 *gobo* root
1 tablespoon vinegar
1 pound Japanese *taro (sato imo),* fresh or frozen
1 tablespoon salad oil
2 cups boneless chicken, cut in 1x2-inch pieces
3 carrots, cut diagonally in slices ½ inch thick
1½ cups chicken stock
1 teaspoon salt
½ teaspoon monosodium glutamate
4 tablespoons *each* soy sauce and sugar
1 can coltsfoot (*fuki*); cut each stalk in half diagonally
1½ cups bamboo shoots, cut in slices ¼ inch thick and roughly 1x2 inches
8 ounces *konnyaku,* cut crosswise in slices ¼ inch thick
16 small dried mushrooms, presoaked
3 tablespoons *mirin*
¼ pound edible podded peas, ends and side strings removed

1. Peel *gobo,* cut diagonally in 2-inch lengths. Cook in water to cover with vinegar for 5 minutes; drain. If you use fresh *taro,* peel and cook in

boiling water for 3 minutes. Cook frozen *taro* 2 minutes, drain.

2. Heat oil in a large kettle and sauté chicken over medium heat for 5 minutes. Add carrots and chicken stock and cook, uncovered, over low heat for 10 minutes. Add the salt, monosodium glutamate, half the soy sauce and half of the sugar, along with *gobo,* coltsfoot, bamboo shoots, *konnyaku,* mushrooms, and *taro.* Simmer uncovered over low heat for 15 minutes. Add remaining soy sauce and sugar and the *mirin,* and cook for 10 minutes. Shake pan occasionally to mix the vegetables.

3. Cook peas in boiling salted water for 2 minutes, drain, and rinse with cold water.

4. Cool *nishime,* then remove vegetables and chicken from the remaining liquid. Arrange in a container piece by piece (include peas also), so each item is separate.

Glazed Smelt

This is a typical Japanese way to preserve small fish. They will keep up to a month in the refrigerator.

2 pounds small (3-inch) smelt
Flour
Salad oil
½ cup soy sauce
⅓ cup sugar
2 teaspoons grated ginger root
1 tablespoon toasted sesame seeds

1. To clean, twist head gently and pull out the head and entrails in one piece, leaving the smelt in perfect shape. Coat with flour, then fry in a small amount of hot oil until crisp, about 10 minutes.

2. Rinse pan and in it put the soy sauce, sugar, and ginger; heat until sugar dissolves. Add smelt to pan, dipping each one in the sauce. Cook over low heat until pan is just about dry and fish are glazed. Sprinkle with sesame seeds.

Japanese food looks like a banquet—even at a picnic.

Crisp Chicken Teriyaki

This can be made with either whole pieces of chicken or bite-size chunks. Because it's as good cold as hot, it's ideal picnic fare.

4 whole chicken breasts, boned and cut in 2-inch squares
2 eggs, beaten
Flour seasoned with salt
Salad oil for frying
½ cup soy sauce
½ cup sugar
1 tablespoon *sake* or sherry
1 clove garlic, minced
1 teaspoon grated ginger root

1. Dip chicken in eggs, then coat with seasoned flour. Heat ½ inch oil in a large frying pan. Cook chicken, half at a time, in hot oil over medium high heat until golden brown, 5 minutes for boned chicken, 20 minutes for larger pieces.

2. Mix together the soy sauce, sugar, *sake,* garlic, and ginger. Dip chicken in sauce, then place on a rack set in a baking pan. Bake in a low oven (250°) until glazed, about 30 minutes.

Rice Balls

These are made with rice, cooked Japanese-style (see page 46).

Wet hands with water, then put about ¼ cup hot cooked rice in your left hand. Close hand slightly so rice will cup in your hand. With your right hand, shape it into a firm ball, a triangle, or an oblong, filling it, if you wish, with *umeboshi* (salted plums) or chunks of Japanese pickles.

If you leave them unfilled, sprinkle with toasted black sesame seeds, or wrap with a band of toasted *nori* (laver seaweed). Cover tightly.

Sushi

For complete directions on preparing *sushi,* turn to page 50.

Hard-Boiled Eggs

Take in the shell, or if you want to be fancy, use a special Japanese egg cutter to give the egg a faceted edge.

Kamaboko

This is a steamed fish cake that is sold in Japanese markets. All you do is slice and eat. The fish cake is white, but depending on the brand, is sometimes tinted tan or cherry-red.

Pickles

Many kinds are available in Japanese markets. If you want to make your own, turn to page 42.

Oriental day hike

For day hikes and backpacking, we never tire of the usual lunch of

When we went on a day hike, one young hiker discovered it was easy to use chopsticks the first time.

salami, cheese, crackers, dried fruit, candies, and nuts. But as I've further explored the world of Oriental foods, I was curious to know if they wouldn't also taste as good when taken out of a pack. The shelves of Oriental markets are crammed with all sorts of intriguing things that would be good on a hike; the difficulty is limiting yourself to buying just what you need.

Trail test

To put the idea to a test, we invited friends who were experienced at hiking, but newcomers to Oriental food. The photographs here might indicate that we fed an army, but we intentionally overdid the menu in terms of variety because we wanted to see how different items would hold up, what the hikers really went for, which foods worked out best.

Normally, you would probably throw most market foods (the dried things) directly into a day pack in their original bags. Because we wanted to try out a variety, we took small amounts from many bags and repacked them in plastic, sealed, foam trays.

Because this is more of a shopping guide than an actual menu, I am not including amount estimates for anything but the cooked foods. How much you take depends on the ages and appetites of the hikers, whether the emphasis is on the hike or the picnic, if it is preplanned or spur-of-the-moment, and how much you are willing to carry. What I did learn from this hike (and what I have discovered repeatedly from all the children who collect in my own kitchen) is that people are willing to try Oriental food and come back for seconds.

ORIENTAL DAY HIKE
Sembei or Arare—Rice Crackers
Dried Cuttlefish
Nori Omelet
Roast Duck, or Chicken Wings with
Oyster Sauce, or
Chicken Legs in Hoisin Sauce
Tofu Salad or Namasu
Fun (fresh rice noodles)
Sweets   Fresh Fruit
Cold Drinks

Sembei or Arare

Once you've opened your eyes and your taste buds to these—in Oriental markets or in the gourmet sections of supermarkets—you may never close them again. Some are sweet, some are salty, many are both. Some have strips of *nori* (laver seaweed) around them, some are sprinkled with sesame seeds.

Many are not crackers at all. You'll find parched or fried green peas or soybeans, *miso* peanuts—and to me, a source of amazement—bagfuls of peanuts with each peanut individually tied with a tiny band of *nori.*

For appetite appeasers

My feeling is that you can't have too many of these. One of our favorites is dried cuttlefish, which we buy shredded in small cellophone bags. (In Japan, this is what we munched on at movies instead of popcorn.) It tastes rather like jerky. Look also for cuttlefish seasoned with *uni* (sea urchin) or small whole cuttlefish dried on a stick. Wafer-thin rings of smoked octopus are another chewy treat.

Nori Omelet

Take this (see recipe on page 73) if the day is not very hot. Pack it close to the cold drinks.

For protein

You can buy ducks and chickens in Chinatown, roasted and ready to go.

Chicken Wings with Oyster Sauce

Follow recipe on page 71.

Chicken Legs in Hoisin Sauce

Prepare this a day in advance.
**10 chicken legs
⅓ cup *hoisin* sauce
¼ cup soy sauce
2 tablespoons sugar
1 clove garlic, minced
1 teaspoon grated ginger root
½ teaspoon salt**

Marinate chicken legs for 1 hour in a mixture of *hoisin* sauce, soy sauce, sugar, garlic, ginger root, and salt.

Place on a rack set over a baking pan. Bake in a moderate oven (350°) until tender, about 50 minutes.

Tofu Salad

Soybean cake is perishable. It will hold up on a cool morning in the woods, but don't leave it out for hours in the sun.

**1 pound soybean cake
1 avocado, peeled and cubed
2 green onions and tops, chopped
¼ cup soy sauce**

Cut soybean cake in 1-inch squares, and drain for 10 minutes in a colander. Combine with avocado, onions, and soy sauce. Pack into a container with a tight-fitting lid. Eat with chopsticks or spear with picks.

Namasu

Hikers don't usually take salads, but they appreciate something crunchy. This is meant to be served at room temperature and doesn't add much weight. Follow recipe on page 40.

For fillers

You could take small loaves of French bread, or the rice balls from the picnic menu, or *sushi,* but on this hike I took *fun,* a fresh rice noodle available in rolled sheets at Chinese markets. Ready-made, it comes plain, or is studded throughout with meat, shrimp, or egg, or is rolled up with a filling.

It's easy to make at home—something the kids enjoy doing. Commercially, it is made with rice flour; at home it should always be made with SWANSDOWN brand cake flour.

Fun—Rice Noodle

Be as careful of this as you are with a potato salad; don't let it sit for hours in the hot sun.

**1 cup unsifted SWANSDOWN brand cake flour
1 tablespoon cornstarch
¾ teaspoon salt
1¼ cups cold water
2 tablespoons salad oil**

1. Mix cake flour, cornstarch, and salt in a bowl. Combine water and oil and gradually pour into the flour, blending until smooth. Pour through a sieve to be sure there are no lumps.

2. Lightly grease a 9-inch pie pan with salad oil and pour in batter to just cover bottom (about ¼ cup); tilt pan to distribute evenly. Place pan on a rack in a steamer and steam until firm, 2 to 3 minutes.

3. Remove pan from steamer (use a hot pad) and set in a baking pan filled with water and ice cubes. This hastens the cooling. Cool for 2 or 3 minutes. Loosen edges with a knife and roll the noodle. Grease the pan again and repeat. Makes 5 to 6 noodle rolls.

To eat plain, cut the noodle roll in 1½-inch slices and dip in soy sauce.

Fun Filling

You can also add flavorful bits of food to the noodle batter before it is steamed; or roll it into the cooked noodle.

**1 tablespoon oil
6 raw shrimp, coarsely chopped
2 dried mushrooms, presoaked, diced (save soaking liquid)
¼ cup diced cooked bacon or barbecued pork
2 tablespoons diced *chung choy* (salted turnip)
1 teaspoon soy sauce
1 green onion and top, chopped
2 tablespoons Chinese parsley leaves
2 tablespoons diced omelet**

Heat salad oil in a frying pan and toss in shrimp and mushrooms. Stir-fry for 1 minute; add 1 tablespoon mushroom soaking liquid, and cook for 1 minute. Add bacon or barbecued pork, *chung choy,* and soy sauce, and cook just until all the liquid has evaporated. Cool; stir in onion, Chinese parsley, and diced omelet. Scatter some of this mixture over each noodle roll before steaming.

For quick energy, something sweet

Chinese markets are full of packaged sweets: strips of candied coconut, winter melon, and ginger, which have been rolled in sugar, and whole candied kumquats; dried fruits such as persimmons, which are both beautiful and delicious. One of our favorites is Japanese *ame,* a candy similar to caramel that is eaten paper and all (the ''cellophane'' is made from edible ingredients). At bakeries you can find steamed sponge cake or winter melon cookies. Don't forget about fortune cookies or almond cookies, available at many supermarkets.

Many Oriental foods are good choices for a day hike or back packing.

Formal Japanese meal

A traditional, formal Japanese dinner is aesthetic, delicious, and tranquil—and lots of work if you serve many guests. The last time I served one, I clocked myself: three hours to set the table and decide on the dishes; four hours and 15 minutes of actual food preparation; and three hours the next day to wash the dishes and put them back. A *niesi* friend who has put on a comparable production says that she gave a marvelous party but didn't have time to eat a bite.

I don't consider four hours a lot of cooking time for a dinner party for eight, but I do consider six hours of taking out and returning the dishes rather impressive. (Not that I minded at all: I loved the challenge of table arrangement and the pleasure of handling pretty things.)

Formality simplified

But the following particular menu is a breeze, and has been vastly scaled down from both the true Japanese dinner and the last one I served. Although it is not as elaborate as you might find in a restaurant, it is aesthetic, delicious, and—of supreme importance to *this* cook—tranquil. Setting the table takes more time than setting it for the Chinese banquet; but, because almost everything is prepared ahead, there is no last-minute cooking scramble.

If you have a very large coffee table, you might want to serve on it, with cushions to sit on. I usually serve at a Western-style table because it is easier for me to set and clear and I figure if my guests are comfortable in their accustomed chairs they are more willing to experiment with new foods.

If you don't want to serve all the food in individual dishes, you could serve part of it on larger dishes in the middle of the table. Provide serving spoons, or do it as the Japanese do; let each guest help himself with chopsticks, turning them over so they serve with one end, eat with the other.

Even with a simple menu, I find it almost essential to keep a list on the refrigerator of what I am serving and what goes with what so I won't forget anything. Soup and salad garnishes and dipping sauces can be prepared early in the day, but that doesn't mean they'll all make it to the table unless I have written a reminder for myself.

> **JAPANESE DINNER FOR 4**
> Suimono
> Sunomono
> Sesame Chicken   Kimpira
> Steamed Rice   Pickles
> Sake   Tea
> Fresh Fruit

Suimono—Soup

4 cups *dashi*
or chicken stock
¼ teaspoon salt
½ teaspoon soy sauce
Dash of monosodium glutamate
½ stalk celery
2 mushrooms (stems removed)
3 slices bamboo shoots
4 edible podded peas

Season *dashi* (recipe page 33) or chicken stock with salt, soy sauce, and monosodium glutamate. Cut celery, mushrooms, bamboo shoots, and peas in matchstick strips. Cook celery, mushrooms, and bamboo shoots in boiling salted water for 2 minutes; add peas and cook 1 minute. Drain and rinse with cold water. To serve, distribute the vegetable garnishes in four soup bowls and pour in hot soup.

Sunomono—Salad

Prepare cucumbers and *sunomono* dressing using the recipe on page 39. Garnish with small cooked shrimp.

Sesame Chicken

2 large chicken breasts
⅓ cup *sake* or sherry
2 teaspoons salad oil
2 tablespoons soy sauce
1 teaspoon vinegar
½ teaspoon sugar
⅛ teaspoon monosodium glutamate
2 tablespoons ground toasted sesame seeds

Split chicken breasts in half; bone and skin. Marinate for 30 minutes in mixture of *sake,* salad oil, soy sauce, vinegar, sugar, monosodium glutamate, and sesame seeds. Place chicken in a baking pan and broil 5 to 7 inches from the heat until you can pierce easily with a fork, about 10 minutes. Baste with marinade several times during cooking. Cut chicken in crosswise slices, then reassemble in the original shape on plates. Garnish with lime wedges.

Kimpira—Vegetable Side Dish

This glazed vegetable combination is good served hot or at room temperature. It is made with *gobo,* a slender brown root that the Japanese cultivate for eating. You may know it as burdock, a common weed. (For ways to grow, see the chapter on vegetable gardening, page 89.) Even

---

after cooking, *gobo* should be slightly crisp.

1 large or 2 small *gobo*, peeled and cut in 2½-inch matchstick lengths
1 tablespoon vinegar
2 tablespoons salad oil
1 large carrot, peeled and cut in matchstick pieces
2 tablespoons soy sauce
1½ tablespoons sugar
¼ teaspoon monosodium glutamate
Dash of cayenne

Soak *gobo* in cold water with vinegar for 15 minutes. Heat salad oil in a large frying pan. Drain *gobo* and sauté for 3 minutes. Add carrot and continue cooking over medium heat for 4 minutes. Add soy sauce, sugar, monosodium glutamate, and cayenne. Continue cooking until vegetables are glazed.

Steamed Rice

See recipe for Japanese-style rice on page 46. Allow 1 to 1¼ cups uncooked rice for 4 persons.

Pickles

For suggestions see page 42, or buy pickles from a Japanese market. Cut pickles in bite-size pieces and serve in small individual dishes.

Sake

This faintly sweet rice wine is served warm, poured from a *sake* jug into tiny cups, and sipped little by little with the meal. To heat, place a filled *sake* jug in a pan and pour in enough water to come half way up the sides of the jug. Heat water to simmering, then turn off heat and let sit several minutes before serving.

Fresh Fruit

Place five large strawberries on each plate with a mound of powdered sugar for dipping, or cut small bananas in diagonal slices ½ inch thick and arrange on small plates so they resemble their original shape. Wedges of melon or pears would be another good choice. Cut the fruit in bite-size wedges, and provide toothpicks for spearing.

Tea

The Japanese usually drink green tea and they drink it plain, without sugar, cream, or lemon. It comes in many different grades. The better the quality the higher the price. One rounded teaspoon of tea to 2 cups of hot water is the usual proportion. You may prefer to use less tea if you brew a larger quantity. Let the tea steep 3 minutes before serving.

A Japanese meal contains many small surprises served in individual dishes.

A Chinese family meal

Cooking and eating habits do change as they pass from generation to generation. In the home shown here, the parents were both raised on Chinese food, occasionally eating American food on weekends. Now their child is growing up eating a Chinese meal two days out of the week.

But that doesn't quite mean that he's eating American foods the rest of the time. To Jeannette, his mother, Chinese food means four or five dishes served on the table at the same time—which, to me, means a Chinese guest dinner. It delights me that she serves Chinese food often as a single dish, but because of her background she doesn't consider that a Chinese dinner, while I serve Chinese food often as a single dish, and because of my background, I *do.*

Jeannette learned to cook from both her mother and her father. Lee is her maiden name; she learned to cook the Lee family's almond pudding as a child.

Although she no longer puts on this big a spread every night, she insists it's a family dinner, not a guest dinner. (The long-time friend who was house guest is considered part of the family.) And she cooked it all in front of me in surprisingly short time, about 1½ hours all told.

When you are two, a soup spoon, fingers, or help from your father is easier than using chopsticks.

It was fascinating to watch her cook. She fried the cabbage all at once, then used part of it in the chicken dish and part of it in the egg pancake. The soup was in a separate pot, as was the rice. The chicken went into a warm oven when it was ready, along with the egg pancake. She continually washed up and re-used dishes as she cooked. And the kitchen was clean when she was ready to serve.

CHINESE FAMILY MEAL FOR 4
Vegetable Soup (with bean cake)
Fu Yu Spareribs
Royal Chicken on Emerald Threads
Bean Sprout Egg Pancake
Stir-Fried Green Beans and Beef
Steamed Rice
The Lee Family's Almond Pudding

This may not be an everyday menu in a Chinese home, but when you invite a good friend to dinner, this is as simple as courtesy (and habit) will allow. The spareribs take care of themselves in the steamer. Cook the chicken first, the egg pancake next, and keep them both warm in the oven while you cook the stir-fried dish at the last minute.

Vegetable Soup
Any homemade vegetable soup would be good, but the Chinese garnish their soup with soybean cake instead of croutons. Cut a generous amount of soybean cake in 1-inch squares and simmer in soup for 3 minutes before serving.

Fu Yu Spareribs

You may want to eat these spareribs with your fingers, but the Chinese way is to hold them with chopsticks in one hand and to hold the rice bowl directly under them with the other. The ribs make a lot of juicy sauce that's good spooned over rice.

1½ pounds spareribs, cut in 1-inch
    lengths
¼ cup *fu yu* (fermented bean cake)
1 teaspoon salad oil
2 teaspoons soy sauce
¼ teaspoon *each* salt and sugar
1 clove garlic, minced
1 slice ginger root, minced
2 teaspoons cornstarch

Trim excess fat from spareribs and cut between the bone. Mix *fu yu,* salad oil, soy sauce, salt, sugar, garlic, ginger, and cornstarch in a bowl that will fit inside the steamer. Put spareribs in bowl and turn several times to coat with the sauce. Steam in the bowl in a steamer for 1 hour; stir once during cooking.

Royal Chicken on Emerald Threads

2 teaspoons sherry
1½ chicken breasts, split in half
    and boned
    Salt and pepper
¼ cup *each* flour and cornstarch
3 tablespoons salad oil
3 cups shredded cabbage
¼ cup sliced onion
1 tablespoon salad oil

    Royal sauce: Mix together 1 table-
    spoon *each* catsup, salad oil, sesame
    oil, sugar, vinegar, and soy sauce.

1. Rub sherry over chicken and sprinkle with salt and pepper. Shake flour and cornstarch together in a paper or plastic bag; add chicken and shake until coated. Heat the 3 tablespoons oil in a frying pan and sauté chicken over medium heat until browned and tender, about 15 minutes.

2. Sauté cabbage and onion in a pan with the 1 tablespoon oil for 5 minutes. Place two-thirds of the cabbage on a serving plate; save the rest for the egg pancake. Cut chicken crosswise in slices ½ inch thick, arrange on cabbage, and spoon over the Royal sauce. Keep warm in a low oven until serving time.

Bean Sprout Egg Pancake

    Salad oil
1 cup bean sprouts
    Dash *each* salt and sugar
2 Chinese sausages, split in half
    lengthwise and thinly sliced crosswise
5 eggs, beaten together with a dash
    of salt and pepper and 1 teaspoon
    water
    Cabbage and onion mixture saved
    from cooking earlier for the chicken

1. Heat wok or frying pan; add 1 tablespoon oil and heat. Add bean sprouts and stir-fry for 1 minute. Sprinkle with a dash of salt and sugar. Remove from pan.

2. Cook sausages in wok over medium heat for 5 minutes; remove from pan and pour off half of drippings.

3. Return wok to medium heat. Pour in half of egg mixture and cook an omelet by lifting up the cooked edges of the egg and letting the uncooked egg run underneath. When egg is almost set, cover the middle with half of the bean sprouts, half of the reserved cabbage, and half of the sausage. Fold omelet in half and transfer to a serving bowl. Repeat, using the remainder of the egg, bean sprouts, cabbage, and sausage. Keep hot in a warm oven until ready to serve.

Stir-fried Green Beans and Beef

½ pound flank steak, sliced across
    the grain in pieces ¼ inch thick
1 teaspoon *each* cornstarch and soy
    sauce
¼ teaspoon *each* salt and sugar
1 clove garlic, minced
    Salad oil for frying
2 green onions, cut in 1½-inch
    lengths
    Salt
1 pound green beans, cut diagonally
    in 1½-inch lengths
2 tablespoons water
2 tablespoons oyster sauce
1 teaspoon soy sauce
1 teaspoon cornstarch mixed with
    2 tablespoons water

1. Marinate meat with cornstarch, soy sauce, salt, sugar, and garlic for 10 minutes.

2. Heat wok or frying pan; add 2 tablespoons oil and heat. Toss in green onion and cook for 30 seconds. Add meat and stir-fry over high heat for 1 minute or until browned on the outside, pink in the middle; remove from pan.

3. Heat 2 more tablespoons oil in wok, sprinkle with salt, add beans, and stir-fry over high heat for 2 minutes. Add 2 tablespoons water, cover, and cook for 1½ minutes. Remove cover and cook 30 seconds. Return meat and onion to pan, add oyster sauce and soy sauce. Stir cornstarch-water mixture to recombine; add to meat and give a quick stir until thickened.

The Lee Family's Almond Pudding

You could cut this recipe in half, but after you taste it, I think you'd be sorry if you did. The pudding is wonderfully smooth and quivers slightly when you spoon into it. Agar-agar, unlike regular unflavored gelatin, sets at room temperature, but because this pudding contains cream, it should be refrigerated. Agar-agar and rock sugar are available in Chinese markets.

1 stick white agar-agar
4¼ cups cold water
½ pound rock sugar
4 cups (1 quart) half-and-half
2 teaspoons almond extract
    Mandarin oranges or maraschino
    cherries for garnish

1. Break agar-agar into pieces and place in a kettle with the water for 1 hour to soften. Boil until agar-agar melts. Add rock sugar, reduce heat to medium, and stirring, cook until sugar dissolves.

2. Cool 5 minutes, then stir in half-and-half and almond extract. Pour into 10 dessert bowls and chill in refrigerator. Garnish with mandarin oranges or cherries. Serves 10.

A meal cooked at the table

If I were eager to put together a whole Oriental meal for guests, and not too confident in my cooking skills, I would serve a meal that is cooked at the table for my first attempt. I didn't do that, but I wish someone had steered me in the right direction.

For this type of meal, everything is prepared or arranged in advance, the equipment requirements are simple, the guests do part of the cooking, and the results are so gratifying that you'll confidently go on to other things. And whether you're aware of it or not, you are, in assembling it, practicing one of the basic techniques of Oriental cooking: the artful arrangement and presentation of food.

Cook it sitting down

There are many Oriental meals that can be cooked at the table—on a griddle, in an electric frying pan or electric wok, on a hibachi if you eat outside. The advantage to the cook is not so much that she doesn't do all the cooking (she often does) but that she does it sitting down, surrounded by company, unharried by worries of getting other courses to the table, because many table-cooked meals are literally one-course, one-plate meals. Somehow, after sitting at the table for an hour or two or three, sniffing and eyeing a parade of foods as they cook, a dessert seems unnecessary, as does a salad or any side dishes. Guests often get their "salad" by snitching from the vegetable trays, anyway.

Centuries old

The methods for table cooking have been around for a long time in many Far Eastern countries. The Genghis Khan dome pictured on the cover and at right (see page 67 for recipe) originated in Northern China and eventually spread to Korea and Japan. Genghis Khan's warriors wore metal hats with slits in them, and legend has it that they used them as cooking grills. In Japan today cooking on this type of grill is called *kabuto yaki* (helmet cooking).

The idea for table cooking probably originated with farmers and fishermen who cooked and served food from a common bowl at the table. One can imagine that the source of heat for cooking warmed the diners as well, in body and in spirit.

Youngsters prepare

It tickles me to think that even after all these centuries, table-cooking still performs some very special functions. One friend, the mother of teenagers, says she counts on it whenever they leave their youngsters home alone to host a dinner party. She cuts up the meat and vegetables in the morning (twice as much as she would serve to adults), lets the girls take charge of arranging them on trays, instructs the boys to take charge of the griddle, and goes out the door with a light heart, knowing that everyone will still be around the table when she comes home. (She has it figured out to an exact science: 10 youngsters at one table griddle give parents exactly enough time to take in a single-feature movie.) What's more, she has few dishes to face, because they don't even use plates, but take the foods directly from the griddle with chopsticks.

Although I present below a menu and recipes for *teppan-yaki* and hot pot, you will do better if you assume there is no true menu or recipe for any kind of table cooking; it's simply a matter of selecting ingredients and mastering a technique.

Cooking on a griddle

Teppan-yaki, cooking on an iron griddle, has become popular in Japanese restaurants both in Japan and America. Customers sit around a large grill and watch the chef put on a first-class show, and eat the food sizzling hot. Strangely enough, although I love this food, I don't particularly enjoy having it in a

Entire meal cooks on Genghis Khan Dome.

restaurant—I feel too rushed. The chef cooks everything so quickly that I feel I have to eat it quickly too. At home, around a pretty table, I relax and enjoy it, cooking and eating at my own pace.

With only one griddle, this type of meal is comfortable for only 4 to 6 people, unless you don't mind spending the whole evening at the table.

TEPPAN-YAKI FOR 4 TO 6
Teppan-yaki   Rice
Dipping Sauce
Roast Chestnuts (optional)
Wine, Beer, or Tea

Teppan-yaki

Almost any vegetable that cooks quickly can be cooked on the griddle. You might include slices of eggplant or yellow summer squash, sweet potato rounds, or edible podded peas. Although the proportions for this dish are flexible, a good balance would be two parts vegetables to one part meat. Serve with one of the dipping sauces below. A small spatula or tongs work well for turning the food.

2 onions, cut in half lengthwise, then cut in slices ¼ inch thick
2 green peppers, cut in ¼-inch-thick rings
½ head Chinese cabbage, cut in 1-inch-thick slices
12 large mushrooms, cut in ¼-inch-thick slices
1 pound bean sprouts, washed and drained
3 zucchini, cut in ¼-inch-thick slices
2 pounds boneless beef, sirloin, tenderloin, or top round
½ cup salad oil
1 cube butter
Salt and pepper
Soy sauce

Arrange vegetables attractively on platters or in baskets, keeping each one in a separate section. Cut meat in slices ¼ inch thick and arrange on platter, or put the meat on a cutting board, bring it to the table, and slice it as needed. Place salad oil in a container that can be used for pouring, such as a small metal tea pot or a pitcher. Place butter on a plate. Arrange the oil, butter, salt, pepper, and a small container of soy sauce on the table near the griddle. Bring the meat and vegetables to the table just before sitting down.

To cook, heat griddle and pour on a little oil. Place part of the meat and some of the vegetables on the griddle. Place a small chunk of butter on top of the vegetables. Sauté until partially cooked, season with salt and pepper and a few drops of soy sauce, turn over, and continue until done. The cabbage and bean sprouts will cook in 2 to 3 minutes, the meat and other vegetables will take a few minutes longer. Cut zucchini and meat in smaller pieces so each person can take a bite at a time. Replenish the griddle as needed.

Rice
Cook Japanese-style (page 46).

Ponzu Dipping Sauce
Mix together ½ cup *each* lemon juice, soy sauce, and chicken stock. Serve in individual bowls.

Mustard Dipping Sauce
Blend until smooth: ½ cup soy sauce, ½ cup chicken stock, and 2 teaspoons dry mustard. Stir in 2 tablespoons ground toasted sesame seeds. Serve in individual bowls.

Roast Chestnuts
Though I seldom serve a dessert with *teppan-yaki,* I would be tempted by chestnuts if they're in season.

Count on 2 or 3 chestnuts per person. Score the skin with X's; arrange on pie tin, one deep. Roast in oven for about an hour at 350°. Pass in a basket.

Cooking in broth
Not all table cooking is done with dry heat. You can cook combinations of vegetables and meat, poultry, or fish in hot-seasoned broth.

For this kind of table cooking, you need a heat source and a container deep enough to hold the liquid. The Mongolian fire pot on page 26 is heated by placing hot charcoal briquets inside the funnel. The moat around the funnel holds the hot stock.

A casserole set over an electric hot plate or alcohol burner is another possible arrangement for this type of cooking, though an electric frying pan would work as well.

As with *teppan-yaki,* the food is cut and arranged ahead of time and brought to the table. Each person picks up the food with chopsticks, adds it to the hot soup, cooks it briefly, then seasons each bite with a dipping sauce. If you are not adept with chopsticks, a fondue fork is a good way to spear the food—and hang on to it as it cooks.

HOT POT FOR 4 TO 6
Hot Pot   Rice
Dipping Sauce
End-of-the-Meal Soup
Wine, Beer, or Tea

Hot Pot
You can cook just about anything in broth as long as it is cut in small pieces. The ingredients listed for *teppan-yaki* would be just as good in hot pot. One of my Chinese friends includes some of the following when she serves a hot pot meal: cubes of soybean cake, thin slices of chicken breast, canned abalone slices, shelled raw prawns, small oysters, strips of flank steak marinated in a little sherry and soy sauce, large thin slices of bamboo shoots, spinach leaves, edible podded peas, and sliced cabbage.

And you can use any kind of broth. Chicken stock is the best all-round broth to use with meat, poultry, or fish. I've made it with *dashi,* too, when I was serving an all-seafood meal.

Dipping Sauce
Thin oyster sauce with a little salad oil, or season soy sauce with a little sugar, vinegar, Tabasco, and a few drops sesame oil. Serve in individual bowls.

End-of-the-Meal Soup
The bonus of cooking in broth is ending up with a marvelously rich soup that you can ladle into cups to drink. If you wish, you can add some cooked rice to the soup along with chopped green onion and two beaten eggs to make an even heartier soup. The Chinese frequently add fresh cooked noodles.

Dining is leisurely and guests sometimes help when you cook a meal at the table.

Ingredients and equipment

You don't need to set up a whole new kitchen to cook Oriental food, but by investing in a few special seasonings you can handle a wider variety of recipes. Stocking a few basic tools will make cooking easier—and more enjoyable.

Each time I watch a shopper in an Oriental market, I marvel at the time and thought that goes into the selection of the plumpest chicken, the freshest fish, the brightest greens. Choosing quality ingredients is basic to cooking good Oriental food. And using the right seasonings is important too, to obtain true Oriental flavor.

Check your cupboard

Many of the recipes in this book can be made with items you already have in your cupboard. But if you treat yourself to a few basic spices, sauces, and seasonings used in Oriental cooking, you'll be able to try a wider range of recipes.

Not all ingredients are rare and unusual or hard to find. An increasing number are showing up in supermarkets or in shops specializing in gourmet foods. A few things can only be bought in a Chinese or Japanese market. (If there isn't an Oriental market in your immediate area, turn to page 30 for a listing of centrally located stores. Some will fill mail orders.) The real puzzle comes in knowing what the food looks like, how it is packaged, and how it is used.

Read the labels

United States government labeling requirements have gone a long way in taking the mystery out of what you are buying. The law requires that labels on prepared foods be printed in English, listing all ingredients in the order of the quantity contained. Many labels, especially on canned goods, include a picture for quick identification, and if you stop to read the small

◁

Labels on Oriental foods may look foreign, but you'll also find the names in English.

print you may even find directions for serving. Don't hesitate to ask if you want to know more. I've always found store owners and customers helpful in sharing ideas and information.

You may wonder about the cost of Oriental ingredients and ask, "Aren't they very expensive?" Fresh vegetables out of season are, and except for an occasional splurge, I can postpone my craving for yardlong beans in the wintertime when they are expensive and buy pea pods which are cheaper—much the same as putting off the temptation to buy strawberries in February.

If Oriental seasonings are new to you, you may question the price of some and your need for them. All I can say is that some imported ingredients are expensive, but a little goes a long way.

Not all of the foodstuffs discussed here are called for in the recipes in this book. But all the information will give you a better understanding of Oriental cooking.

Soy sauce

The one essential ingredient in Chinese and Japanese cooking—probably familiar to most Americans—is soy sauce: a savory, salty, brown liquid made from fermented soybeans, wheat, yeast, and salt. It comes in many grades, types, and degrees of saltiness. Chinese cooks often use two kinds to season one dish—light soy for saltiness, dark soy for color. Most Japanese soy sauce sold in this country is a medium soy. It is slightly sweeter than the Chinese brands; it is also the kind of soy sauce used to test all the recipes in this book.

Soy sauce comes in bottles and cans. If you plan to use it in marinades

that call for large amounts, you'll save money buying it in large cans. It will keep indefinitely at room temperature. Domestic soy sauce, made by a chemical process rather than fermentation, tends to be very concentrated, salty, and slightly bitter.

Soy sauce is truly an all-purpose seasoning, but don't be tempted to overuse it. It was never designed to give an "instant" Oriental flavor to every dish. When cooking vegetables, especially, it is better to season with salt and a *small* amount of soy sauce so the bright or light colors will not be darkened.

Ginger root

Fresh ginger root, a gnarled tan-colored root, is a must in both Chinese and Japanese cooking, and powdered ginger should not be used as a substitute. If you can't find the fresh root, it is better to omit the ginger from a recipe. Cooking brings out the flavor of ginger; it is also used uncooked as a condiment. Peel the ginger root before using (when I am in a hurry and want to grate it, I don't). Keep ginger root in the refrigerator; the skin will dry but it will stay fresh inside. You can also freeze it whole. Grate while still hard and frozen. Another method of storing is to break the root into small chunks and keep in the refrigerator in a jar filled with sherry.

Sesame seeds

Toasted sesame seeds are used in so many Oriental dishes that you would do well to toast a large quantity at one time. Put seeds in a frying pan and heat over medium heat until they begin to jump. Turn out of pan immediately; cool, and crush or grind. Japanese markets sell a small plastic grinder just for sesame seeds. You fill it with the toasted seeds and grind as you need them.

Oils, vinegars, and wines

Cooking oil is important, especially in Chinese cooking, since so many dishes are stir-fried or deep-fried. Some cooks prefer peanut oil, but I find any vegetable-based salad oil works without imparting its own flavor to food. Olive oil is the one exception. Because of its distinctive flavor, I feel it has no place in Oriental cooking.

Oil can be used several times for deep-frying. Filter the oil by pouring it through a paper towel fitted inside a sieve. Keep in the refrigerator in a covered container. Before using it the next time, brown several slices of ginger root and a green onion in the oil to remove odors.

Sesame oil, made from white sesame seeds, is not used for frying, but to give fragrance to dishes. The flavor is so strong only a few drops are required in most recipes. It is usually added last.

Chinese markets sell chili oil, which is used as a seasoning, frequently with noodle dishes.

So many vinegars are available that if you bought them all it might be equal to setting up a small wine cellar. But the flavors are different, delicious, and interesting to try. Chinese cooks generally use a white rice vinegar to make pickles. Red vinegar goes into sweet and sour sauces, dressing for chicken salad, and general cooking. A thicker black vinegar, made from black rice (similar to brown rice) is used in very special dishes such as pickled eggs or pickled pigs feet—and is thought to be particularly nutritious for new and expectant mothers.

The slightly sweeter Japanese white rice vinegar is my preference for Japanese-style salads and *sushi*. American distilled white vinegar and cider vinegar can be used but are slightly stronger and more pungent in flavor.

Sake, Japanese rice wine, is served slightly warmed with meals and is also an important seasoning ingredient in Japanese cooking. It is often available in American liquor stores. *Mirin,* sweet *sake,* is used only for seasoning. Several kinds of Chinese rice wine are sold for drinking or seasoning. For general cooking, you can substitute sherry or any white table wine.

Japanese sauces, seasonings, and pickles

An incredible array of bottled sauces are sold in Japanese markets and supermarkets. For example, besides soy sauce, you can find a low-sodium soy sauce (for specialized diets), *sukiyaki* sauce, *teriyaki* sauce, and soup base for noodles. Most of these are used in cooking and you will find recipes in this book on how to prepare your own. Other flavoring sauces include *tonkatsu* sauce (to serve with pork cutlet), *ponzu* sauce (used as a dip for grilled seafood or meat), and *ikari* sauce (another sauce to serve with meat).

Furikake, which comes in a shaker-type bottle, is a kind of seasoning to sprinkle over rice and noodles. It is made primarily from seaweed and there are many flavor variations. Japanese pepper spice also is good on noodles and adds a special pungency.

If you want to take a shortcut making *sushi,* look for a dehydrated seasoning for *sushi* that you mix with the cooked rice.

Bottled, canned, and refrigerated pickles range from sliced lotus root, *umeboshi* (salted plums), pickled ginger root, *rakkyo* (pickled scallions), *takuan* (pickled *daikon*), and *kim chee* (Korean pickled cabbage), as well as more familiar vegetables.

Chinese sauces, seasonings, and pickles

After opening the following sauces, store in the refrigerator; they will keep indefinitely.

Oyster sauce is a thick, brown sauce made from oysters, soy sauce, and brine. Despite the name, it has very little fishy taste. It is sold in bottles and cans and is used as a condiment like catsup. It is also used for cooking such dishes as broccoli beef with oyster sauce.

Hoisin sauce is a thick, sweet, brownish-red sauce made from vegetables and spices. It is used as a condiment with dishes such as *mu shu* pork or roast duck, and is often an ingredient in a marinade for poultry.

Plum sauce, spicy and pungent, is similar to a mild chutney. It is frequently served as a condiment with chicken or duck.

Many other Chinese sauces based on beans come in cans or jars and a spoonful can be used to flavor pork, fowl, or steamed fish. For Cantonese-style cooking, one of the most widely used is brown bean sauce (sometimes labeled bean sauce or ground bean sauce). For Szechwan-style cooking, which is hotter and spicier, you can buy a can of Szechwan bean sauce (moderately hot), sweet bean sauce (more spicy than sweet), hot bean sauce, and extra hot bean sauce with chili.

If hot, spicy food is your preference, look for jars of sesame seed paste, chili paste with garlic, and preserved radish with chili. All of these seasonings can be used in small amounts to give zest to Chinese or American food.

Fermented black beans are used as a seasoning for meats, fish, poultry, and vegetables, usually in combination with garlic. After opening, store them in a jar with a tight-fitting lid (they *do* have a strong odor). Before using, put the beans in a sieve and rinse to remove the excess salt.

Chung choy (salted turnip) is used in Chinese cooking to flavor soups, and steamed meat and fish. It is sold in plastic bags. Repack after opening —to contain the odor. The turnip will never spoil; the salt preserves it forever. If you like a spicier flavor, look for salted turnip seasoned with chili. Try it in cooking, or slice off bits and eat.

Chinese five-spice powder is a combination of ground anise seed, fennel, clove, cinnamon, and brown peppercorns and is sold ready-mixed in small cellophane bags. You can also buy star anise, a star-shaped whole anise which contains seeds in each petal. It is used crushed, broken, or whole to flavor meat or poultry.

Szechwan pepper (speckled brown peppercorns) has a mildly hot flavor and a pleasant aroma. Use it in stewed or braised dishes and to season duck. You can also make a pepper-salt to use as a table seasoning. Heat whole peppercorns in a pan until browned, about 1 minute. Crush with a mortar and pestle and combine one part crushed pepper and two parts salt.

Dried tangerine peel, used to flavor soups, meat, and poultry, is sold by the ounce. The older the skin the more prized and expensive it is. Before using, soak in water for 30 minutes, then scrape off and discard the inside (white part) of the peel.

Lotus seeds are small, delicately flavored water-lily seeds used to prepare duck and winter melon soups.

Red dates (jujubes) are small, dried, reddish fruit with wrinkled skin. Add to soups or stews to impart a subtle sweetness.

Chinese mixed pickles, sweet mixed ginger, *sub gum,* (all the same thing) are sold in jars. They can be eaten cold as a garnish or relish, or used in cooking to make sweet-sour sauces.

Sweet cucumber, also known as tea melon, is an amber-colored squash preserved in honey and spices. Use chopped, as a condiment, or slice and steam with pork dishes.

Bean cake—fresh and fried
Soybean cake is almost as much a staple in Oriental cooking as rice. It has a mild flavor, is high in protein, low in cost, and comes in dozens of different forms.

The regular Japanese-style soybean cake is *tofu,* the Chinese style is called *dow-foo,* but there are other varieties—softer, firmer, and even dried. Fried soybean cake comes in small cubes, squares, and oblongs. Fresh soybean cake will keep in the refrigerator for a week; just cover with cold water and change the water daily. Refrigerate fried soybean cake, *without* water, in a plastic bag, or freeze it for longer storage.

Fermented bean cake, also called red bean curd, white bean curd, or *fu yu,* is another form of soybean cake and comes in jars. This is used as a seasoning and should not be substituted for fresh or fried bean cake.

Miso, used primarily in Japanese cooking, is also made from soybeans. It comes in cartons and tubs. Many varieties and brands are available, from the pungent brown and red to the mild-flavored white. *Miso* is used to make soup, dressings for vegetables, and to season meat or fish.

Vegetables— fresh, canned, and dried
For an identification of some fresh vegetables that may be new to you, see the photograph on page 88. Many are also sold dried, canned, and frozen. Processed vegetables often have a slightly different texture and flavor from the fresh ones, so when you substitute a canned vegetable for a fresh one, you don't always end up with the same results.

For example, several varieties of lotus root are grown. One is crisp and usually sold fresh; the other has a higher starch content and is canned and dried. Although the flavors are similar, the textures are completely different.

Bean sprouts change character too in processing and I feel that canned bean sprouts are a poor substitute for fresh ones. If you can't find fresh ones, you might want to try sprouting your own. Place 2 tablespoons dried mung beans in a Mason jar, fitted with a screen lid cut to fit under the screw band. Fill with water and soak overnight. In the morning, drain through the screen, turn jar on its side, and put in a dark cupboard. Immerse in water 2 or 3 times a day and drain. Do this until sprouts appear—usually in 3 to 4 days. Refrigerate until used.

I find fresh water chestnuts irresistible when they are in season. They have a sweet flavor similar to that of fresh coconut. Canned water chestnuts are also good, just as crunchy, and always available.

Bamboo shoots are also usually found in cans. After opening, water chestnuts and bamboo shoots will keep for a week in the refrigerator. Change water daily to prevent souring. I like to store them in glass jars so I can see them and remember to change the water.

Japanese markets carry a greater variety of frozen Oriental vegetables than Chinese markets do, such as soybeans and *taro.* These vegetables are very similar to the fresh ones.

Dried ingredients
Dried mushrooms are probably one of the most expensive Oriental ingredients to buy, but they stretch a long way. For general cooking, any kind and size of Oriental dried mushroom will impart the same delicious flavor, so I look for bags of small ones or broken pieces when a recipe calls for mincing or chopping. For certain dishes I splurge with large whole mushroom caps. Soak the mushrooms in cold water for 30 minutes before using. Always discard the stems.

Cloud ears are another type of fungus sold in Chinese markets. They are crisper in texture than a mushroom. Soak for 30 minutes before using (they will increase a great deal in size).

Dried lily buds, sometimes called golden needles or tiger lily buds, are about 2 to 3 inches long. They have a delicate musky taste, are highly nutritious, and inexpensive. Soak in water 30 minutes before using. They are often used in combination with cloud ears.

Foods from the sea
You'll find a wide selection of these in both Japanese and Chinese markets—such things as scallops, oysters, abalone, squid, octopus, and clams are sold fresh, dried, canned, and salted. Dried fish and dried shrimp are used for broths and to flavor vegetables. Japanese stores sell many kinds of seaweed, from the thick sheets of *kombu* to thin sheets of *nori.* You will find suggestions for using them throughout the book.

Dried Oriental foods offer a colorful collage of texture.

Oriental cooking equipment

If I were setting up a kitchen for Oriental cooking and had to limit my equipment, I would buy a wok, a cleaver, and a Japanese vegetable slicer. I would make do with whatever else I had, and then, because my original selection left out so many fascinating and useful things, I would make a list of the extras for birthday presents.

To cook Chinese and Japanese food, it is not essential to have all the equipment shown on this and the following page. Many Oriental cooks produce culinary feats of magic with a few simple tools, relying on their skills to produce the magic rather than a battery of pots and pans. But for me, the extras make cooking easier and a lot more fun. And for meals cooked at the table, I find it hard to resist the beauty of some of the cooking equipment and containers.

One at a time

There is an advantage to buying equipment one piece at a time. It allows you to concentrate on learning to use the equipment, see how it works for you, and perhaps even discover that it will serve a multiple purpose. But no matter what you buy, you won't enjoy it unless you take it out of the box and use it enough times so it seems like an old friend.

Years ago my first attempts at stir-frying were most discouraging. I had purchased a too-small wok with a round bottom and I had to balance the wok on an adapter ring. This would have been fine on a gas stove but on my electric stove I couldn't get enough heat for flash cooking. (I hadn't learned the trick then of not over-crowding the pan.) After several half-hearted attempts I wondered why the Chinese thought the wok was so versatile, covered it with tile, and used it as a bird bath.

My second attempt was much more successful. I had learned the basics of stir-frying and when I received a wok as a gift I was determined to put it to good use—which I did on special occasions. Because the gift was from one of my children I was frequently asked why I didn't use it more often. That settled it. I took it out of the pantry for good, hung it on a hook where it was accessible, and soon found that I no longer needed all those other pots and pans that crowded my cupboards.

Ways with a wok

You can use a wide frying pan for stir-frying, but a wok has several advantages. Less cooking oil is needed because there is less area to be covered. The curve of the wok keeps the food tumbling back into the hottest spot as you cook, and the high smooth sides reduce the amount of food that ends up on the stove instead of in the pan. You can use a wok for deep fat frying too, and you need far less oil than you would in a flat pan. With the addition of bamboo steaming trays, or a rack and

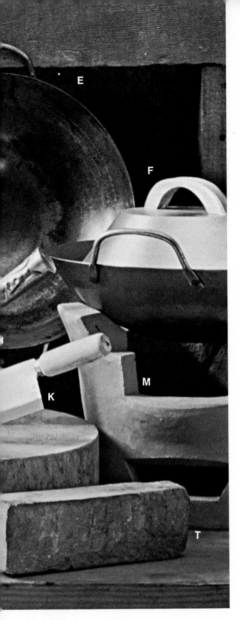

a cover, the wok can be used as a steamer.

The wok was originally designed with a round bottom so it would fit over a clay brazier and get the maximum heat from minimum fuel. To stabilize this kind of wok on a stove, set it inside an adapter ring that sits around the heating element. The ring can be turned with either the wide side or narrow side up. This method is fine on a gas range but not completely satisfactory when you cook with electricity. For electric stoves it is easier to use a wok with a slightly flat bottom so it can sit directly on the heating element. This allows you to get the high heat necessary for stir-frying. When you stir-fry on an electric burner, turn the heat to high and don't turn it down until you finish cooking. If the food starts to burn, lift the wok off the heat momentarily. For steaming or deep fat frying with a considerable amount of oil, use the adapter ring to stabilize the wok, no matter what kind of heat you use. Then

there won't be any chance of spills.

A 14-inch wok (measure across the diameter of the top rim) is the ideal size for the average family. A 12-inch wok is fine when cooking for two, but does not adapt as well to other uses, and a 16-inch wok or larger may be too heavy, especially after it is filled with food. Remember, you can always stir-fry a small amount of food in a large wok, but never stir-fry lots of food in a small one.

Woks come in two styles: one with metal loop handles on both sides, the other with a single long handle. The two-handle pan is less likely to tip but the handles get hot and you need to use potholders. Many cooks prefer the single handle as it is easier to lift the pan and pour out the cooked food. There is also some variety in the curvature of the wok. I prefer the deeper kind because the sides confine the splatter—but it is purely a matter of taste.

The most common metal for woks is rolled steel. It transmits heat well but rusts easily. If you have a rolled steel or cast-iron wok, it should be seasoned before its first use to keep food from sticking. To season, wash the wok thoroughly with hot water and soap or detergent; rinse, and wipe dry. Place over medium heat to dry off any excess water, then wipe the surface with a paper towel soaked with salad oil. Continue heating and wiping the surface with oil until the paper towel wipes clean. To clean the wok after each use, fill it with hot water and scrub away any food particles with a stiff brush or a plastic scouring pad. Don't use soap or an abrasive material; this will destroy the surface created by the seasoning process. Be sure to dry the wok thoroughly each time after use or it will continue to rust, and don't be alarmed when it starts to burn black. It is supposed to, and that's when you'll know you are becoming a seasoned cook.

Woks made of stainless steel are satisfactory, and though they are easier to clean they are somewhat less effective as heat conductors.

A lid may come with the wok or you can buy one separately. Because of its shape—a high dome—it is a useful accessory, especially for steaming.

An iron spatula designed to fit the curvature of the wok and a ladle are two other accessories that you might find useful. They are inexpensive and rather crude. Although I find the handcrafted look appealing, I feel that any large metal spoon works as well.

A brass wire strainer with a bamboo handle comes in many sizes, from 4 to 12 inches in diameter. The larger one is probably more useful. It is good for removing big pieces of food from a pan, such as a whole chicken or fish, as well as retrieving tiny particles from the oil when frying.

Long wooden chopsticks are often sold with woks, and once you learn to use them you'll find how useful they are—especially when cooking with hot oil because they do not conduct the heat.

Tools for cutting

I could never limit myself to one knife and I have favorite knives that I use for different cutting jobs. But for all-round cutting and chopping, a Chinese cleaver is one of the best, whether you are cooking Oriental or American food. I use it to cut, slice, dice, and mince meat and vegetables; to chop poultry through the bone into smaller pieces; and to crush garlic with the broadside of the blade, which makes for easier peeling and mincing. It also serves as a scoop to lift all the bits and pieces from the cutting board to the pan.

Cleavers come in several weights. For home use, No. 3 (the number is printed on the blade) is considered the best weight, but you should hold it in your hand and get the feel of it before you buy one.

Some cleavers are made of stainless steel, but I prefer those made of carbon steel. Carbon steel blades stain with use and rust if you don't dry them thoroughly, but a carbon steel blade holds a better edge than most stainless steel blades.

Japanese knives, also made of carbon steel, are excellent for slicing, boning, and chopping and you may find them easier than a cleaver to handle. All of these knives, like the cleaver, are surprisingly inexpensive. I would be lost without one of the smaller knives, used for shredding green onions, lemon peel, anything in very fine strips; and the long, thin-bladed *sashimi* knife used to fillet and skin fish with a minimum of waste. A word of caution. The Japanese knives pictured on page 28 are fine for boning but are not designed to chop *through* bones.

No matter what kind of knives you use, treat them with care. Don't soak them in water and don't put them in the dishwasher. Wipe the blade with a hot soapy cloth or sponge and rinse after each use, then dry.

Be good to yourself and keep a sharp edge on your knives. Since much of Oriental cooking is in the preparation, you'll be discouraged before you get the food in the pan if you work with a dull knife.

Chopping blocks

A partner to a cleaver or knife is a surface on which to do all the cutting, mincing, and slicing. Many Chinese restaurant chefs favor a round chopping block—which is nothing more than a good thick slice of hardwood. The cross-cut end of the wood provides the cutting surface and the knife bites into the wood (instead of bouncing off) and facilitates rapid slicing.

The thickness of the block adds several inches height to the level of the chopping surface, so unless you can set it on a table lower than normal counter height, you may find it uncomfortable for extended use. I prefer to use a lighter weight cutting board that I can easily pick up when I want to dump sliced vegetables or meat directly into a pan. A wooden cutting board should be washed with hot soapy water, especially after cutting fresh meat, and dried before putting it away.

Vegetable slicers

You might consider the Japanese slicer a non-essential, but I find it indispensable. Because of its adjustable blade I can slice cucumbers, carrots, daikon, potatoes, zucchini, turnips—any firm vegetable— quickly and consistently thin or thick. I also use the slicer to shred thin slivers of onion, lettuce, and white or red cabbage as a garnish for meat, fish, and salads. For shredding daikon or carrot, use the comblike shredding blade that comes with the slicer. In Japanese cooking the appearance of the food and the way it is presented are important. To me shredded daikon can do wonders as a garnish even for rather plain food—much more fun than parsley. One of the reasons I like the slicer is that it is so fast to use I feel like a professional chef.

For grating daikon and ginger root I use a small Japanese grater, available in ceramic or metal. Any grater will work but the Japanese grater has the advantage of not getting plugged since there are no holes. It is also good for grating citrus peel.

Equipment for steaming

Another Chinese utensil that is not absolutely essential, but that I find particularly handsome, is the bamboo steamer. You can buy sets of baskets that fit into each other, as many as three or four at a time, so several different dishes can be steamed at once when set in a wok filled with water. The baskets come in several different sizes; a basket with a 12-inch diameter is a good size for a 14-inch wok. Bamboo steamers are imported from Taiwan and Hong Kong and vary slightly in size, so if you plan to buy one, buy a top and bottom—or as many layers as you think you will want—at one time and be sure they fit inside each other before leaving the store.

Aluminum steamers are widely available and quite good, and some Japanese hardware stores sell an aluminum steamer with a bamboo lid.

A steamer, however, is easy to improvise. Place a round cake rack inside a wok, or place a rack or plate inside any large kettle with water in it. The rack or plate should stand at least 2 inches above the level of the water. For supports, use custard cups or several tin cans of the same size (tops and bottoms removed). The cover should be 1 or 2 inches above the cooking food so steam can circulate. For example, if you want to steam a large fish, place the fish on a platter, then set the platter on tin-can supports inside a roasting pan. A clean dish towel placed under the cover absorbs the water that collects under the lid.

Efficient non-essentials

An electric rice cooker is a great convenience if you cook rice often. I resisted buying one for years because I felt that I could cook rice as well as an electrical appliance could. I did, but I spent needless time cleaning the stove when the pot boiled over. If you consider investing in a rice

cooker, a four- or five-cup size is best—good for either family meals or entertaining.

Japanese markets also sell a special rimmed saucepan for cooking rice on a conventional stove. The lid fits tightly down inside a rim which catches any water that might boil over.

A Japanese rice paddle is useful for serving rice. It also serves as a good stirring tool when cooking in a pan with a nonstick finish.

Japanese cooks use other specialized pieces of cooking equipment too. Rolled omelet (see page 73) is made in a tamago-yaki nabe (rectangular omelet pan) though I've made it also in a square electric frying pan. With a round pan you just trim off the edges.

A suribachi (Japanese mortar) is a pottery bowl with rough grooves inside. It comes with a surikogi (wooden pestle).

A sudare is an inexpensive bamboo mat used to roll sushi (see page 52), but you could also use a bamboo place mat to do the job.

Japanese cooking equipment:
A. Earthenware pot (Donabe), **B.** Electric rice cooker, **C.** Aluminum cooking pot, **D.** Electric hot plate (single burner stove), **E.** Serrated bowl (Suribachi) and wooden pestle (Surikogi), **F.** Teapot, **G.** Cast iron pan for sukiyaki (Sukiyaki-nabe) or tempura, **H.** Grater, **I.** Slicer/shredder with changeable blades, **J.** Plastic cutting board, **K.** Knife for boning, **L.** Knife for boning meat or chopping vegetables, **M.** Knife for slicing vegetables or boneless meats, **N., O.** Knife for slicing sashimi or other fish, **P.** Rectangular omelet pan (Tamago-yaki nabe), **Q., R.** Skimmer, **S.** Cooking chopsticks, **T.** Rice paddle (Shamoji), **U.** Cooking chopsticks, **V.** Bamboo skewers, **W.** Bamboo mat.

Bamboo skewers come in many sizes and are good for skewering chunks of meat, poultry, fish, or shellfish to cook on a grill, hibachi, or under the broiler. They are less apt to burn if you soak them in water for a few minutes before using.

Cooking-at-the-table equipment

There are so many handsome things available for table cooking, it's difficult to say which kind is best. For grilling at the table an electric griddle is ideal. For table barbecuing, you could use a hibachi, a Genghis Khan dome over a barbecue, or a clay brazier, or even a large clay flower pot filled two-thirds full of sand. Place hot coals on the sand and cover with a square of hardware cloth for a cooking surface. For one-dish meals cooked in broth, an electric frying pan or saucepan will work. A casserole set over an electric hot plate or alcohol burner is another possible arrangement.

When burning charcoal indoors, be sure the room is well ventilated. Charcoal releases carbon-monoxide and breathing a large quantity will make you feel groggy or ill.

If you are further tempted, here is a rundown on some of the other equipment available.

✓Mongolian fire pot or Chinese hot pot. This is generally made of brass. It is heated by placing hot coals inside the chimney (start the charcoal briquets outside in a heavy bucket, then transfer to the chimney with tongs.) The moat around the chimney holds the hot stock. Small wire strainers are usually used to scoop the cooked food from the broth but you could use chopsticks or fondue forks *instead.*

✓*Sukiyaki-nabe.* When heated over an electric hot plate, this cast-iron pan is used for *sukiyaki.* By adding a wire draining rack, it can also serve as a cooker for *tempura.* This type of pan is heavy and thick (in order to maintain an even heat) and is generally used for dishes that require only a small amount of liquid. Other iron pots of greater depth are available for dishes using large amounts of broth. Before using an iron skillet the first time, wash it with hot water and soap or detergent; rinse, fill with water, and boil for 15 minutes. Empty and rinse. Always dry an iron pot well before storing so it won't rust.

✓*Donabe.* Japanese potters turn out a beautiful assortment of earthenware pots *(donabe)* that can be used for serving food at the table or for table cooking. Those that are glazed both inside and out are generally designed for ovenware and are probably most practical for all-round cooking. However, don't place them over direct heat.

Other pottery, glazed on the inside *only,* can be used over an electric hot plate for table cooking. Despite their heavy appearance, these pots are rather fragile; never start cooking in them over high heat, and never place an empty pot on the heat. Avoid getting the outside, especially the bottom, wet. They should be heated and cooled slowly as any sudden change in temperature is likely to cause cracking.

Sources for food and utensils

Many Oriental food products are sold in supermarkets and gourmet shops, with serving dishes and cooking equipment often found in department stores and import shops. If looking for rare items, check Yellow Pages for Oriental Shops.

At the time of printing, the following stores carry canned and dried Oriental foods; a few stock fresh foods and most carry dishes and utensils. Because policies differ and managements change, check the stores nearest you to determine what they have in stock and how best to buy it. Except where noted, all stores will fill mail orders.

East
Yoshinoya
36 Prospect St.
Cambridge, MA 02139
Emphasis on Japanese food products, utensils.

Kam Kuo Food Corp.
7 Mott St.
New York City, NY 10013
Oriental food products, dishes, utensils.

Kam Man Food Products, Inc.
200 Canal St.
New York City, NY 10013
Emphasis on Chinese food products, dishes, utensils.

A C Gifts New York, Inc.
2642 Central Park Ave.
Central Plaza Shopping Center
Yonkers, NY 10710
Oriental food products, dishes, utensils.

Meidi-ya
18 N. Central Park Ave.
Hartsdale, NY 10530
Emphasis on Japanese food products, dishes, utensils. No mail orders.

Oriental Food Mart
909 Race St.
Philadelphia, PA 19107
Oriental food products, utensils.

Bando Trading Co.
2126 Murray Ave.
Pittsburgh, PA 15217
Oriental food products, dishes, utensils.

Mikado Grocery
4709 Wisconsin Ave., N.W.
Washington D.C. 20016
Emphasis on Japanese food products, dishes, utensils.

Midwest
Franklin Food Store
1309 E. 53rd St.
Chicago, IL 60615   No mail orders.
Oriental food products, dishes, utensils.

Oriental Grocery
18919 W. 7 Mile Road
Detroit, MI 48219
Oriental food products.

The First Oriental Food, Inc.
1517 Como Ave. S.E.
Minneapolis, MN 55414
Oriental food products, dishes, utensils.

Oriental Lee Foods, Inc.
7051 Maple St.
Omaha, NE 68104
Oriental food products, dishes, utensils.

Soya Food Products
2356 Wyoming Ave.
Cincinnati, OH 45214
Oriental food products, dishes, utensils.

South
Tonyee Imports
7539-A Dadeland Mall
Miami, FL 33145
Oriental food products, dishes, utensils.

Oriental Imports
54 North Orange Ave.
Orlando, FL 32801
Oriental food products, dishes, utensils.

Asian Trading Co.
2581 Piedmont Road N.E.
Atlanta, GA 30324
Oriental food products, limited utensils.

Abrigo Oriental Foods
552 S. Fifth
Louisville, KY 40202
Oriental food products, dishes, utensils.

Oriental Mart
11236 Florida Blvd.
Baton Rouge, LA 70815
Oriental food products, limited dishes, utensils.

Kim's Mart
606 Keman Ave. South
St. Louis, MO 63130
Oriental food products, dishes, utensils.

Edo-ya
223 Farmers Branch Shopping Center
Dallas, TX 75234   No mail orders.
Emphasis on Japanese food products, dishes, utensils.

Asiatic Import Co.
821 Chartres St.
Houston, TX 77003   No mail orders.
Oriental food products, dishes, utensils.

West
New Meiji Market
1620 W. Redondo Beach
Gardena, CA 90247   No mail orders.
Oriental food products, dishes, utensils.

Modern Food Market, Inc.
318 E. Second St.
Los Angeles, CA 90012
Emphasis on Japanese food products, dishes, utensils.

Easy Foods Company
299 Castro St.
Mountain View, CA 94041
Oriental food products, limited dishes, equipment.

American Fish Market
1790 Sutter St.
San Francisco, CA 94115
Emphasis on Japanese food products.

Ginn Wall Co., Inc.
1016 Grant Ave.
San Francisco, CA 94133
Chinese dishes, cutlery, utensils.

Soko Hardware Company
1698 Post St.
San Francisco, CA 94115   No mail orders. Oriental dishes, utensils.

Pacific Mercantile
1925 Lawrence St.
Denver, CO 80202
Oriental food products, dishes, utensils.

Tokyo Oriental Grocery Store
Kietzke Plaza, Kietzke and Moana
Reno, NV 89503   No mail orders.
Oriental food products, dishes, utensils.

Anzen Importers
736 N.E. Union Ave.
Portland, OR 97232
Oriental food products, dishes, utensils.

Sage Farm Market
1515 S. Main
Salt Lake City, UT 84115
Oriental food products, dishes, utensils.

Uwajimaya Inc.
519 6th Ave. South
Seattle, WA 98104
Oriental food products, dishes, utensils.

The language of Oriental cooking

Most labels on packaged Oriental foods are printed in English. If you cannot find an item and ask for it by name, it is often easier to use the Chinese or Japanese name. The following glossary will help identify both food products and names of dishes which you may cook yourself or order in a restaurant. A few less frequently used English words are also included. On words where pronunciation may be a problem, a guide is given (in parentheses) following the word.

Aburage (ah-boo-rah-gay). Fried soybean cake.

Agar-agar. A gelatinous product made from seaweed, used as a thickening agent.

Age-zushi (ah-gay-zoo-shee). Fried soybean cake filled with *sushi* rice.

Aka miso (ah-kah mee-so). Red soybean paste.

Arare (ah-rah-ray). Rice cracker.

Beni shoga (ben-nee show-gah). Red pickled ginger root.

Bok choy. Chinese mustard cabbage with dark green leaves on fleshy white stalks.

Buta dofu (boo-tah doe-foo). Pork with soybean cake.

Cee gwa. Luffa gourd, also known as *cing gwa*, *sin gwa*, and Chinese okra. Eaten as a fresh vegetable when young, or dried and used as a sponge.

Cellophane noodles. Transparent noodles made from dried mung beans. Frequently called bean threads.

Char siu. Chinese barbecued pork.

Chawan mushi (cha-whan moo-shee). Japanese steamed custard containing meats, fish, or vegetables.

Chow mein. Chinese stir-fried dish of various combinations of vegetables and meats served over fried noodles.

Chuka soba (choo-kah so-bah). A kind of precooked instant noodle.

Chung choy. Preserved salted turnips used as flavoring.

Chung fa. Multiplying or green onions.

Chungshan. District in southern China where a dialect of Cantonese is spoken.

Dai gai choy (die-guy-choy). Sharp-flavored mustard cabbage. Also sold as India mustard or broadleaf mustard cabbage.

Daikon (die-kohn). Japanese white radish.

Dasheen. Hawaiian variety of *taro*, grown for the edible starchy tubers.

Dashi (dah-shee) Japanese soup stock made from dried kelp and shaved, dried bonito, used to flavor many dishes.

Doan gwa. Large Oriental gourd, also known as winter melon, used primarily for soups.

Dobu (doe-boo). "River ditch" or "wet dirt"; a curing mash for Japanese pickling.

Donabe (doe-nah-bay) An earthenware pot used in Japanese cooking and serving.

Donburi (dohn-boo-ree). "Big bowl"; Japanese rice served in a large bowl with various toppings.

Dow foo pok. Fried soybean cake.

Dow gauk. Yardlong or asparagus bean. Also called Chinese long bean.

Foo gwa. An Oriental gourd, known as bitter melon, with a flavor to match its English name.

Foo yung. Chinese omelet.

Fuki (foo-kee). A perennial; the stem is eaten as a vegetable. Also known as coltsfoot or butterbur.

Fun. Chinese fresh rice noodles.

Fun see. Chinese name for cellophane noodles.

Furikake (foo-ree-kah-kay). Seasoning for rice and noodles.

Furoshiki (foo-roh-shee-kee). Square of fabric tied so the corners form a handle for use as a carryall.

Fu yu (foo yoo). Fermented soybean cake, used as a seasoning.

Gai choy (guy choy). Light-flavored mustard cabbage. Also sold as India mustard or Chinese mustard greens.

Gai lohn (guy-lohn). Oriental broccoli-like vegetable.

Gobo (goh-boh). Slender brown root cultivated for Japanese cuisine; also known as burdock.

Gow choy. Chinese chives.

Harusame (hah-roo-sah-may). Japanese name for cellophane noodles.

Hasame yaki (hah-sah-may yah-kee). Broiled eggplant with chicken.

Hashi (hah-shee). Japanese chopsticks.

Hibachi ((hee-bah-chee). A small Japanese charcoal stove or grill.

Hin choy. An Oriental green vegetable with small fuzzy leaves.

Hoisin. Thick, slightly sweet Chinese sauce made from a soybean base.

Ho lan do. Edible podded peas; also called sugar peas or snow peas.

Hosomaki (hoh-soh-mah-kee). *Sushi* rice made into a small roll, usually wrapped with seaweed *(nori).*

Ikari sauce (ee-kah-ree). Flavoring sauce to serve with meat.

Instant noodles. Precooked packaged noodles, ready to eat.

Kabuto yaki (kah-boo-toh yah-kee). "Helmet cooking"; descriptive phrase for cooking on a metal domed grill.

Kamaboko (kah-mah-boh-koh). Japanese fish cake.

Kampyo (kahm-pyo). Dried gourd strips.

Kare (kah-reh). Curry.

Katsuobushi (cah-tsoo-o-boo-shee). Dried bonito shavings used to make basic soup stock. Shavings also sprinkled on food as a garnish.

Kim chee. Korean pickled cabbage.

Kimpira (kim-pee-rah). Japanese vegetable dish made with burdock.

Kitsune-zushi (kee-tsoo-nay-zoo-shee). *Sushi* rice stuffed in fried soybean cake. See *Age-zushi.*

Kombu (kohm-boo). Dried kelp, a species of seaweed.

Kombu maki (kohm-boo mah-kee). Pieces of kelp rolled, tied with dried gourd strips, and simmered in a broth.

Konnyaku (kohn-yah-koo). Stiff jelly-like food made from the starchy tubers of the devil's-tongue plant.

Lop cheong. Chinese sausage.

Mai fun (my-fun). Vermicelli made from rice; puffs up instantly when fried.

Mao gwa. Small winter melon.

Mein. Chinese noodles, available fresh or dried.

Mirin (mee-rin). Sweet Japanese rice wine *(sake)* used in cooking.

Miso (mee-so). Red or white soybean paste.

Miso shiru (mee-so shee-roo). Japanese soup made from *miso* and broth.

Miso-yaki (mee-so-yah-kee). Broiled food that has been marinated in a soy-bean paste-based sauce.

Mitsuba (mit-soo-bah). Japanese parsley.

Monosodium glutamate. A white, crystallized, flavor-enhancing agent.

Mu shu pork (moo-shoo). Chinese pork and egg dish, usually folded inside a thin Mandarin pancake.

Mizutaki (mee-zoo-tah-kee). Japanese boiled chicken with vegetables.

Nabe (nah-bay). A Japanese cooking pot.

Namasu (nah-mah-soo). Raw vegetables marinated in a Japanese dressing.

Niban dashi (nee-bahn dah-shee). Strong version of *dashi*, resulting from a second boiling of kelp and bonito.

Nigiri-zushi (nee-gee-ree-zoo-shee). Tokyo-style hand-shaped *sushi* rice.

Niku nabe (nee-koo nah-bay). Family-style version of *sukiyaki.*

Nira (nee-rah). Japanese name for Chinese chives.

Nisei (nee-say). Second generation Japanese.

Nishime (nee-shee-may). Cooked vegetables with chicken.

Nori (noh-ree). Laver seaweed.

Norimaki (noh-ree-mah-kee). *Sushi* rice made into a large roll, wrapped with *nori.*

Nuka (new-kah). Rice bran used in Japanese pickling process.

Oshiwaku (o-shee-wah-koo). Wooden mold for pressing *sushi* rice.

Oshi-zushi (o-shee-zoo-shee). Pressed *sushi* rice mixture.

Oyako donburi (o-yah-koh dohn-boo-ree). Big bowl of rice topped with chicken and egg.

Pak choy. Another name for *bok choy.*

Panko (pahn-koh). Japanese dried bread crumbs.

Ponzu (pone-zoo). Sauce used as a dip for grilled seafood or meat.

Poo gwa. Large Oriental squash resembling a baseball bat.

Rakkyo (rah-kyoh). Pickled scallions.

Ramen (rah-men). A kind of instant noodle.

Rice sticks. See *Mai fun.*

Saba (sah-bah). Mackerel.

Sai fun (sigh fun). Another name for cellophane noodles.

Saimin (sigh-min). Hawaiian version of precooked instant noodles.

Sake (sah-kay). Japanese rice wine.

Sansho (sahn-show). Prickly ash leaves, a Japanese pepperlike herb. used as a garnish.

Sashimi (sah-shee-mee). Sliced raw fish.

Sembei (sem-bay). Rice crackers.

Shamoji (shah-moh-jee). Paddle for serving rice.

Shio zuke (shee-o zoo-kay). Japanese salt pickles.

Shirataki (shee-rah-tah-kee). Japanese noodles made from yams.

Shiro miso (shee-roh mee-so). White soybean paste.

Shiso (shee-so). An annual; leaves used for seasoning in Oriental cooking.

Shogoin (show-go-in). Japanese turnip.

Shoyu (shoy-yoo). Japanese soy sauce.

Shungiku (shoon-gee-koo). *Garland* chrysanthemum.

Siew choy. Slightly sweet-tasting variety of Chinese cabbage.

Soba (soh-bah). Tan or tea-flavored Japanese buckwheat noodles.

Somen (soh-men). Very thin Japanese noodles.

Sub gum. Chinese mixed sweet pickles.

Sudare (soo-dah-ray). Bamboo mat used for rolling *sushi.*

Suimono (soo-ee-moh-noh). Clear Japanese soup, attractively garnished.

Sukiyaki (soo-kee-yah-kee). Beef and vegetables cooked in a small amount of broth.

Sumiso (soo-mee-so). Japanese dressing or dipping sauce for cold vegetables.

Sunomono (soo-noh-moh-noh). "Vinegared things"; specifically a dressing for cold vegetables.

Suribachi (soo-ree-bah-chee). Serrated bowl used for grinding or mashing; a mortar.

Surikogi (soo-ree-koh-gee). Wooden pestle used with *suribachi.*

Sushi (soo-shee). Japanese delicacy made with vinegared rice.

Takuan (tahk-whan). Japanese pickled *daikon.*

Tamago-yaki nabe (tah-mah-go-yah-kee nah-bay). Rectangular Japanese omelet pan.

Taro. Tropical plant grown for its tuberous starchy edible root; also known in Japanese as *sato imo.*

Tempura (tem-poo-rah). Seafood and vegetables deep fried in batter, served with dipping sauce.

Teppan-yaki (teh-pahn-yah-kee). Cooking on an iron griddle.

Teriyaki (teh-ree-yah-kee). Japanese barbecue; meat, poultry, or fish marinated in a sauce and broiled on a grill.

Tofu (toh-foo). Soybean cake in a number of forms.

Tonkatsu (tone-cot-soo). Japanese pork cutlet.

Udon (oo-dohn). Thick, white, Japanese noodles.

Umeboshi (oo-may-boh-shee). Japanese salted plums.

Uni (oo-nee). Sea urchin.

Wakame (wah-kah-may). A variety of seaweed.

Wasabi (wah-saw-bee). Very hot Japanese horseradish, available in powdered form, made into paste by addition of water.

Wok. A large curved pan of steel with high smooth sides for stir-frying, deep fat frying, or steaming.

Ya choy. A variety of Chinese cabbage.

Yaki-nori (yah-kee-noh-ree). Toasted seaweed.

Yaki soba (yah-kee so-bah). A type of instant noodle.

Yakitori (yah-kee-toh-ree). Small pieces of chicken skewered and grilled over a charcoal fire or broiler.

Yin and *Yang.* Chinese term for contrasting harmony in nature.

Yuen sai. Chinese parsley.

Soups and stocks

Most Chinese start dinner with a light, clear soup.
The Japanese often approach soup as you
would approach a centerpiece. Many of these soups
take longer to garnish than they do to cook, and many
will introduce you to exotic new flavors.

Most Oriental soups are served as part of a meal, not as a whole meal. They go together quickly, without long hours of simmering at the back of the stove as our soups do (or as our grandmother's soups did). The first reaction of many Americans to an Oriental soup is that "It didn't fill me up." It isn't supposed to.

But in their home countries, "prelude" or "first course" isn't quite their function either—at least not always. A soup can show up at various points during a Chinese dinner, and sometimes two or three different soups appear at two or three surprising times during a banquet. The Japanese often serve a bowl of soup alongside their main course. It's one more taste contrast, one more treat for the eye, one more option for picking and choosing.

Soup as a meal

Some of these recipes can easily serve as full-meal soups. Dried *bok choy* soup was designed with this in mind. With *won ton* soup or winter melon soup, all you have to do is provide more soup per person. Many of the *miso shirus* will welcome extra meat or vegetables or *tofu* or egg. And if "soup" to you means only a rich, filling, noodle soup, turn to page 46. You'll find some recipes there that might be noodle soup to you, but are just noodles to the Japanese.

◁

Japanese soups (clockwise from top left); White miso *soup with clam, Chinese chives; Clear soup with carrot, daikon, potato, chicken, green onion; Red* miso *soup with tofu, green onion top; Clear soup with watercress bundle, mushrooms; Clear soup with shrimp, sansho leaf; Clear soup with spinach bundle, lemon peel.*

Japanese soups

The cornerstone of Japanese soup—as well as of sauces, noodles, and most traditional cooking—is *dashi*. It is used in *suimono,* the clear soups, and in the thicker soups, *miso shiru*. Our closest counterpart is chicken or beef stock.

The difference is that *dashi* is a fish stock, not a meat stock. The fish flavoring is delicate, fragile, suggestive. What makes many Americans sit up and blink the first time they read a recipe for *dashi,* is to learn that it is made with *kombu*—dried kelp—as well as fish.

To me, *dashi* has a wonderful richness. It imparts mysterious undertones and subtle overtones to dozens of my favorite dishes. Without it, the dominant flavor of most Japanese food would be sugar and soy sauce.

If you resist fish and kelp, feel free to substitute chicken broth for *dashi* in any recipe in this book. I often do so myself—for the sake of speed. When I do, I prefer a homemade or canned broth; they're richer in flavor than bouillon cubes.

Instant dashi. Few cooks today make *dashi* from scratch. Our local Japanese market no longer carries shaved bonito because even their regular Japanese customers prefer the simplicity of instant *dashi*. It comes in jars, or in boxes containing foil packets—even in bags like tea bags. Most brands are very good, and all carry directions in English.

I hope, though, that you'll try making your own *dashi* at least once. Once you have the ingredients on hand, its not all that far from being "instant." And the ingredients keep in the cupboard, so you can always have a supply on hand.

Suimono

Suimono is the soup that appears often in sets of colored slides of Japanese food: a clear broth, in a small handsome bowl, with snippets of colorful, shapely, picturesque foods floating on the surface. It's pretty as a picture because the Japanese approach it as a picture.

Like all creative works, it requires a bit of forethought. I often spend more time with the garnish than I do with the broth, happily. It's fun to try something new, and it's fun to be surprised. Some things fan out. Some things curl up. Some things *sink*. Not

---

Dashi—Basic Japanese Soup Stock

1 square (4-inch) *kombu* **(dried kelp)**
6 cups water
¾ cup *katsuobushi* **(shaved dried bonito)**

Wash kelp with damp cloth. Place in a saucepan with water, and heat just until large bubbles appear. (Remove kelp immediately or the flavor will be too strong.) Add shaved bonito, turn off heat, and let stand until shavings settle to the bottom of the pan. Strain. Use or store.

Dashi—both instant and homemade—is best when fresh, but you can cool, cover, and refrigerate it for as long as 2 days. Economical Japanese housewives reuse the kelp and bonito by putting them in a pan with 5 cups water and boiling for 5 minutes. The result is somewhat stronger than the original *dashi,* and is called *niban dashi*.

bok choy or edible podded peas in the chicken stock before pouring it over the *won ton*.)

Deep-fried won ton. If you make up the whole batch at once, with only a few people to feed, you may want to deep-fry a few—to eat along with the soup, or to freeze. Cook in hot vegetable oil (375°) until golden brown, and drain on paper towels. To freeze, (when cool) pack in plastic bags or coffee cans. To reheat, place on cookie sheets and bake, while still frozen, in a 350° oven for 12 to 15 minutes.

The traditional way to serve deep-fried *won ton* is with a sweet-and-sour sauce, but we prefer a cocktail sauce. To make, mix 1 cup catsup with 1 tablespoon lemon juice, 1 tablespoon Worcestershire, ½ teaspoon sugar, and 1 tablespoon chopped green onion.

Hot Sour Soup

There are many versions of hot sour soup. This one has a light, peppery taste.

> 4 cups chicken stock
> ¼ pound boneless pork, cut in matchstick pieces
> 4 dried mushrooms, presoaked and thinly sliced
> ½ cup matchstick slices bamboo shoots
> 10 medium-sized raw prawns, shelled and deveined
> 1 teaspoon soy sauce
> ½ teaspoon salt
> 1 teaspoon sherry
> 2 tablespoons white vinegar
> ½ teaspoon white pepper
> ½ soybean cake, cut in 1-inch cubes
> 2 tablespoons cornstarch mixed with ¼ cup water
> 2 eggs, slightly beaten
> 1 teaspoon sesame oil
> 2 green onions and tops, cut in 1½-inch lengths and shredded

1. Bring chicken stock to a boil and add pork; reduce heat and simmer 5 minutes. Skim foam from the top.

2. Add mushrooms, bamboo shoots, prawns, soy sauce, salt, and sherry; simmer 5 minutes. Add vinegar, pepper, and bean cake, and continue cooking 3 more minutes.

3. Stir cornstarch water mixture (to recombine) and pour into soup. Stirring gently, cook 1 minute or until soup thickens slightly. Keep stirring and slowly add eggs until they form long threads. Taste; add more salt if necessary. Stir in sesame oil and sprinkle with green onions. Serves 6.

Sizzling Rice Soup

This is too ticklish and time consuming to serve to guests, but my family doesn't mind assembling for last-minute tensions and theatrics.

Rice Crust

> 1 cup long-grain rice
> 4 cups water
> 1 teaspoon salt

Combine rice, water, and salt in a heavy pan. Cover, bring to a boil, and simmer 30 minutes. Drain.

Spread rice thinly and evenly on greased cookie sheet. Dry in 250° oven 5 to 6 hours, turning as it becomes golden-brown.

Soup

> 6 cups chicken stock
> ½ cup diced chicken breast
> ¼ cup bamboo shoots
> 6 *each* sliced water chestnuts and fresh mushrooms
> 1 teaspoon sherry
> 6 edible-podded peas, ends snapped and strings pulled

Heat chicken stock in saucepan with chicken breast, bamboo shoots, water chestnuts, mushrooms, and sherry. Simmer 5 minutes; add small slices of pea pods and cook 1 minute longer.

To assemble: This is the tricky part because you need to have the rice crust, the soup, and the soup bowl all hot at the same time. Heat soup bowl by filling with boiling water. Pour 1-inch of salad oil in a heavy pan; turn the burner to medium high (375°). Fry pieces of oven-dried rice until golden brown.

Drain soup bowl, fill with piping hot soup, and carry to the table. Slide the hot rice into the soup. If your timing is right, it really will sizzle. Serves 6.

Winter Melon soup

Soup steamed and served in a whole winter melon is a flamboyant way to start any meal. When I do it, I do it for guests, to make a big splash, with the largest melon I can find. For steaming, it *must* be mature. Size is no clue; look for frosty white wax on the skin.

When you buy it by the slice, to cook as a vegetable or *in* a soup, the age of the melon doesn't matter.

This soup is so unusual to serve to guests I feel it is worth growing winter-melon at least one time if you can't buy one. (See vegetable gardening chapter for growing instructions.)

Winter Melon Pond Soup— for Company

Steaming a big melon takes logistics. I improvise a steamer by placing a dishtowel on the bottom of a canning kettle, with custard cups on top to support a rack. If the melon thrusts its head over the top, I cap it with a basket, draped with towels. It's unorthodox, but it works.

> 8 dried mushrooms
> 1 piece dried tangerine peel, about 1½ inches in diameter
> ½ cup dried lotus seeds (optional)
> 1 winter melon, 12 to 15 pounds
> 2 cups diced raw chicken meat
> 2 cups diced raw pork
> ½ cup diced ham (trim off fat)
> ½ cup diced bamboo shoots
> ⅓ cup diced water chestnuts
> ½ cup canned ginkgo nuts
> 1 tablespoon soy sauce
> 2 teaspoons salt
> Chicken stock (approximately 8 to 10 cups)

1. Soak mushrooms, tangerine peel, and lotus seeds in water for 30 minutes. Slice mushrooms and remove stems. Scrape off inside of tangerine peel.

2. Wash winter melon and scrub peel with a stiff brush to remove waxy surface. Cut off top and reserve; scoop out seeds and stringy portions.

3. Set melon in a bowl or in the middle of a dishtowel (which will act as a sling.) Place on a steaming rack in a large kettle. Put mushrooms, tangerine peel, lotus seeds, chicken, pork, ham, bamboo shoots, water chestnuts, ginkgo nuts, soy sauce, and salt inside of the melon. Heat chicken stock and pour inside melon to fill three-fourths full. Stir once to separate diced meat.

4. Put top on melon and add water to kettle to come to bottom of steaming rack. Cover and steam for 3 or 4 hours or until melon meat is tender.

5. Lift melon out of kettle with the sling and carefully transfer to a large chop plate. Remove tangerine peel. Taste; and add salt if necessary. Spoon some of the soft melon out and mix with soup when serving. Serves 8 to 10.

Winter Melon Soup—for a Family Meal

> ¾-pound-slice winter melon
> 4 cups chicken stock
> 1 piece dried tangerine peel, about 1 inch in diameter, presoaked and scraped
> 3 dried mushrooms, presoaked and thinly sliced
> 4 water chestnuts, cut in half and thinly sliced
> 2 teaspoons soy sauce
> 1 egg, slightly beaten (optional)

1. Peel winter melon, scrape away seeds and stringy portion, and cut crosswise in ¼-inch-thick pieces.

2. Bring chicken stock to a boil and add melon, tangerine peel, mushrooms, water chestnuts, and soy sauce. Simmer for 15 minutes or until melon is soft. Taste and add salt if necessary. Add egg and stir until it cooks in long threads. Serves 4 to 6.

1. Carve uncut melon a day ahead. Cut off lid and fill just before cooking.

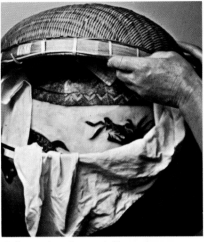

2. Improvise steamer with any large kettle. Melon sits on dishtowel sling.

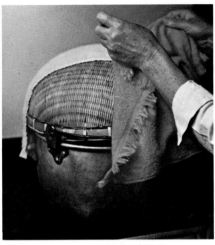

3. Cap top of melon with basket. Drape with towels to hold in the steam.

Winter Melon Pond Soup is a flavorful show stopper, even if you don't carve the melon.

Salads, dressings, and pickles

To think "Oriental salads and pickles," you must empty your mind of lettuce, Roquefort, dill . . . Making an Oriental salad is more a matter of cutting, cooking, and marinating the vegetables that we most often eat hot. Oriental pickles are made from *daikon,* eggplant, turnips, and cabbage, as well as cucumbers.

Few salads as we know them in America are served with an Oriental meal. This chapter contains recipes for some of the exceptions. You will note that all of them are based on vegetables. You will also note that few of the vegetables are served raw.

Although both the Chinese and Japanese use a great abundance of vegetables, they usually cook them—very briefly—before serving them, even if their function in the meal is a cold side dish. Some vegetables are salted and squeezed. This technique draws out the natural moisture. The vegetables are crisp but the raw taste is gone. The difference in what one's palate expects and accepts was pointed out by one of our Chinese friends who said that her father found it very strange to eat many uncooked vegetables—the flavor was just too uncivilized.

Serving temperature

Most Chinese vegetable dishes are served hot. You will find them in the next chapter. But sometimes the Chinese marinate, chill, and serve vegetables as part of a cold plate. I like to serve these chilled bites as appetizers, either in small bowls as a finger food, or arranged in variety on a platter with chopsticks for each guest. Somehow each crisp bite seems to taste better if you have to negotiate for it with chopsticks.

The Japanese are less fussy about the temperature of their vegetables, serving them more often at room temperature than hot or chilled. Per-

◁

Individual Japanese Salads. Top: Asparagus with Sumiso Dressing, page 39. Left: Bamboo Spinach, page 40. Right: Shungiku with Sesame Dressing, page 40.

haps this is a matter of expedience only, but you might find that the custom grows on you; because the flavors don't share the spotlight with temperatures, they seem much more assertive.

Don't think that these are just cold, leftover vegetables. Indeed, they are quite special. The flavors are fresh, the colors bright, and the delicate sauces add subtle undertones.

Appetizers

Many of these Oriental "salads" can be used as interesting appetizers, served on a platter as finger food to be passed with drinks. However, because they take so well to picture-pretty arrangements, I prefer to serve them in individual bowls as a first course. And, of course, you can also serve them as the Japanese most often do: as a side dish with the main course.

Pickles, which are covered later in this chapter, can also be served as appetizers. The Orientals like them best as an accompaniment to rice. As you will see, an Oriental pickle is seldom a cucumber.

Sunomono Dressing

I like this best over cucumbers; Japanese cooks do too, but sometimes they use it with carrots and *daikon* (instructions below). It is a good way to give a Japanese flavor to a tossed green salad or a mixture of shredded red and white cabbage.

    1 cup vinegar
    ½ cup sugar
    1 teaspoon salt
    ½ teaspoon monosodium glutamate

Combine all ingredients in a saucepan and heat just long enough to dissolve sugar. Cool. Store in refrigerator and use as needed.

Cucumbers

If you have space in your garden for cucumbers, consider planting one of the Oriental varieties.

The long, thin-skinned seedless cucumbers are excellent, too, and are appearing in markets more often these days. If you can find only the thick-skinned variety, be sure to peel them, leaving a few narrow strips of green for color.

Cut cucumbers in paper-thin slices. Sprinkle with salt (1 teaspoon for each cucumber) and rub salt into the cucumbers. Let stand 30 minutes. Squeeze out liquid, or put cucumbers into a colander and press out liquid.

Place cucumbers in a bowl and sprinkle with a spoonful of *sunomono* dressing; rub dressing in. Let stand 15 minutes. Squeeze again. Mound on individual plates or bowls. Sprinkle with a few more drops of dressing before serving. Consider garnishing with crab meat, shrimp, or canned abalone.

Carrot and Daikon

Shred vegetables. Soak in cold water for 30 minutes. Drain and combine with enough dressing to moisten lightly.

Sumiso Dressing

This is worth playing around with. It's good as a dipping sauce for an individual vegetable served as a first course (see photograph, left), good as a dressing over an arrangement of one or two vegetables served as a salad, and good as a dip with an assortment of vegetables served as appetizers.

It takes to many vegetables, including asparagus spears, broccoli, cauliflower, carrots, edible podded peas, zucchini strips, green beans, and green onions. Do not overcook the vegetables; they should remain crisp and crunchy. Drain immediately after cooking and rinse with cold water to stop cooking and prevent discoloration.

2 tablespoons vinegar
2 tablespoons sugar
¼ cup white *miso*
¼ teaspoon monosodium glutamate

Blend all ingredients until smooth. If lumps remain, push mixture through sieve. Keep in refrigerator. For a spicier version, blend in 1 teaspoon dry mustard and 2 teaspoons toasted sesame seeds.

Sesame Dressing

When I am trying to "go Japanese" I serve this over *shungiku* (garland chrysanthemum). See photograph bottom of page 38. When I want to perk up a Western meal with an unusual salad, I serve it over spinach or green beans. When I am simply hungry for this particular dressing, I serve it over any cooked vegetable that I have on hand.

Cook spinach or *shungiku* in boiling water 2 minutes; cook beans 4 minutes. Drain, rinse with cold water, and cut in 1-inch lengths.

2 teaspoons toasted sesame seeds
2 teaspoons sugar
½ teaspoon monosodium glutamate
2 tablespoons *dashi* (see page 33) or
**   chicken stock**
½ cup soy sauce

Grind sesame seeds; combine with other ingredients. Or whirl all ingredients in a blender. Enough for 1 pound vegetables.

Sesame-Soy Dressing

This is the traditional dressing for "bamboo spinach" (instructions below)—bundles of spinach resembling bamboo shoots pushing up through the ground. See photograph page 38.

⅓ cup *dashi* or chicken stock
⅔ cup soy sauce
¼ teaspoon monosodium glutamate

Combine all ingredients.

Bamboo Spinach

Wash 2 bunches spinach (2 pounds) well, leaving bunches attached at the roots. Parboil 2 minutes, drain, and rinse with cold water. Divide into 4 parts; arrange so leaves, stems, and roots are parallel. Gently squeeze to remove all water. Trim off roots. Cut diagonally in 1½-inch lengths.

To serve, dip top of only half the spinach bundles in toasted sesame seeds, about 1 tablespoon. Stand 2 bundles—one with sesame seeds,

one without—in each small serving bowl. Sprinkle *katsuobushi* (shaved bonito) or tiny cooked shrimp at base, about ⅓ cup altogether. Pour small amount of dressing into bottom of each bowl. Makes 8 servings.

Another Sesame Dressing

We're asparagus fans, so anything that tastes good with asparagus is a favorite at our house. For this, I roll-cut the asparagus in 1-inch lengths, parboil for 3 minutes, and let the asparagus chill in the dressing for 30 minutes.

½ cup soy sauce
¼ cup vinegar
1 teaspoon sugar
1 teaspoon toasted sesame seeds

Combine all ingredients. Enough for 2 pounds asparagus.

Spicy Dressing

I like this best with asparagus spears, which is the way I first tasted it. But it's interesting with almost any cold, cooked vegetable I could name, and maybe some raw ones too.

⅓ cup soy sauce
¼ teaspoon cayenne pepper

Combine soy sauce and cayenne pepper.

Creamy Dressing

I call this my *nisei* (second generation) dressing; the mayonnaise certainly didn't come from an old-country kitchen. It's especially good with broccoli, green beans, or cauliflower, cooked and cold.

1 tablespoon toasted sesame seeds
½ cup mayonnaise
2 tablespoons soy sauce

Grind sesame seeds; mix with mayonnaise and soy sauce. Or whirl all ingredients in a blender.

Namasu

This is a cross between a pickle and a salad. I usually serve it as an appetizer with this selection for low-calorie crunching: cucumbers, strip-peeled and thinly sliced; onions, thinly sliced; celery and carrots, cut in matchstick pieces; and turnips, halved and thinly sliced.

⅓ cup brown sugar
¾ cup vinegar
1 cup water
1 tablespoon salt
½ teaspoon monosodium glutamate

Combine all ingredients in a pan and heat long enough to dissolve sugar. Cool. Pour over vegetables and refrigerate for at least 24 hours before serving.

Photos show steps for Chinese Chicken Salad. Use fingers to shred chicken.

Smear shredded chicken in roasting pan to soak up flavor of the drippings.

Shred green onions and tops. It is quick work if cleaver has a sharp edge.

Fry rice sticks. Wire strainer makes it easy to remove them before they burn.

Chinese Chicken Salad looks festive when assembled at the table. Spoon over hoisin dressing, top with crisp rice sticks.

Dressings for Uncooked Vegetables

Though these three dressings would all be good over almost any vegetables, I use each so often in certain salads that I am including the salad recipes below. Each dressing recipe makes enough for its partner-salad.

Dressing I

6 tablespoons salad oil
¼ cup rice vinegar
   or mild white vinegar
1 teaspoon salt
⅛ teaspoon *each* white pepper and
   monosodium glutamate
½ teaspoon sugar

   Combine all ingredients. Stir until smooth. Makes ⅔ cup.

Dressing II

2 tablespoons soy sauce
2 tablespoons vinegar
1 teaspoon dry mustard
3 tablespoons salad oil
2 teaspoons sesame oil
2 teaspoons sugar
   Dash monosodium glutamate

   Combine all ingredients. Stir until smooth.

Dressing III

3 tablespoons vinegar
1 tablespoon sugar
1 tablespoon soy sauce

   Combine all ingredients. Stir until smooth.

Chinese Cabbage Salad

Split 1 head (about 2 pounds) Chinese cabbage in half lengthwise; remove core by making a V-shape cut at each stem end. Line a shallow bowl with 8 leaves. Trim curly edges (save to toss in a green salad another night) from stalks; cut stalks into matchstick pieces. Chill in ice water at least 1 hour. Drain and toss with Dressing I. Mound in bowl. Garnish with 2 hard-cooked eggs, sliced, and 1 cup flaked crab or shrimp. Serves 8.

Oriental Meat and Vegetable Salad

Poach half a large chicken breast in lightly salted water, 15 minutes; drain. When cool enough to handle remove skin and bones. Pull into lengthwise shreds.

   Beat 2 eggs well and fry in 2 or 3 thin sheets; cut in lengthwise strips. Cut 4 slices ham in 3-inch-long strips. Strip-peel 1 cucumber, cut in 3-inch lengths, and cut in thin strips. Slice ½ head Chinese cabbage thinly.

   Spread a layer of the cabbage on a serving plate. Arrange four rows on top, one each of the chicken, eggs, cucumber, and ham. At the table, pour Dressing II over salad and stir together before serving. Serves 6.

Turnip Bundles

Cut I turnip crosswise in wafer-thin slices. Cut 1 carrot into 1½-inch lengths and slice thinly. Sprinkle with a little salt; let stand 30 minutes. Squeeze out liquid. Marinate for at least 4 hours in mixture of ½ cup vinegar, 2½ tablespoons sugar, and 1 teaspoon salt. To prepare turnip bundles, take 5 to 6 shreds of carrot from marinade and wrap a slice of turnip around them. The turnip will surround the carrots and stick to itself. Repeat, using all the turnips and carrots.

   Combine in large bowl 1 cucumber, cut in thin rounds; 2 tomatoes, peeled and cut in wedges; and ½ to 1 cup shrimp or other cooked seafood. Pour Dressing III over all; toss lightly.

   Distribute in individual bowls. Garnish with turnip bundles. Serves 8.

Sweet Dressing

Japanese cooks might make this sweeter still, but I've reduced the amount of sugar to satisfy palates long accustomed to sharp-flavored dressings. Among other things, it's delicious over a chilled combination of bean sprouts and watercress. Parboil the bean sprouts 30 seconds; drain and rinse with cold water. Cut watercress in 1-inch lengths.

3 tablespoons rice vinegar
   or mild white vinegar
1 tablespoon sugar
¼ teaspoon salt
⅛ teaspoon monosodium glutamate
1 teaspoon crushed toasted sesame
   seeds

   Combine all ingredients except sesame seeds. Stir until sugar is dissolved. Sprinkle sesame seeds over top of vegetables.

Hoisin Dressing

Delicious on many things—vegetables, meats, fish—and outstanding on Chinese Chicken Salad (below). This salad is a bit of a production, but I think it's worth it, for special people or special occasions.

2 tablespoons *hoisin* sauce
2 tablespoons lemon juice
3 tablespoons salad oil
1 tablespoon sesame oil
2 teaspoons sugar

   Combine all ingredients. Stir until sugar dissolves.

Chinese Chicken Salad

Place 3-pound broiler fryer, split, in roasting pan. Rub all over with mixture of 3 tablespoons *hoisin* sauce, 1 tablespoon soy sauce, ¼ teaspoon *each* garlic salt and salt, and dash of pepper. Place chicken skin-side up, in a roasting pan, tucking 3 green onions, cut in 1-inch lengths, under it. Roast at 350° until tender, 50 minutes to 1 hour.

   When cool enough to handle, remove skin and cut in thin slivers. Pull meat from the bones and, with your fingers, shred enough meat to measure 3 cups. This is easier to do if you don't let the chicken become completely cold. Spoon off half the grease from pan; stir to blend remaining drippings. Smear shredded chicken around in drippings. You can do this part a day ahead.

   Fry rice sticks according to directions on page 49. Thinly slice 1 head iceberg lettuce. Cut 2 green onions (including tops) into 1½-inch lengths. Break ½ cup Chinese parsley into 1-inch sections.

To assemble, place lettuce on a large platter. Top with the chicken, green onions, and parsley. Pour *hoisin* dressing over all before serving. Pass rice sticks in a bowl to be sprinkled over the top. Some cooks toss the rice sticks with the salad, but they wilt quickly in the dressing. For an even crunchier version, sprinkle a handful of cashews or peanuts over the top. Serves 6.

Kimisu Dressing

This goes well with almost any vegetable. Serve it over a combination of shredded cucumber, matchstick strips of celery, and peeled tomato wedges. Or use it as a topping for cooked broccoli and garnish with strips of boiled ham. When I want to serve something really special, I use it in a cucumber and salmon appetizer (below).

1 egg yolk
2 tablespoons water
3 tablespoons rice vinegar or
 mild white vinegar
1 tablespoon sugar
½ teaspoon cornstarch
¼ teaspoon salt

Combine all ingredients in a small saucepan. Stir until smooth. Continue stirring and cook over very low heat until it thickens slightly. Makes ½ cup.

Cucumber and Smoked Salmon Appetizer

The easiest way to shape this is with the special wooden mold shown on page 53. You can improvise by using the lid of a box roughly 4 by 7 inches and at least 1 inch deep. Punch a hole in each corner with a skewer so juices can drain.

1 large or 2 medium thin-skinned
 cucumbers (3½ cups, sliced)
1 tablespoon salt
2 to 3 tablespoons pickled ginger
1 package (3 oz.) smoked salmon,
 thinly sliced
½ cup *kimisu* dressing (above)

Peel cucumbers, leaving a few narrow strips of green peel, and slice thin. Sprinkle with salt. Let stand 30 minutes. Turn into a colander, rinse with cold water, and press liquid out.

Fit plastic film inside mold, leaving 6-inch margins on two opposite sides. This will serve as a sling for easy removal. Arrange one third of cucumbers evenly on bottom of mold; sprinkle with ginger. Place another third of cucumbers over ginger, and cover with a single layer of salmon. Top with remaining cucumbers.

Fold plastic film over the top and cover; if you are using a box lid, cover

Paper thin slices of cucumber form a mosaic on Cucumber and Smoked Salmon Appetizer. Top with Kimisu Dressing.

with the bottom of the box. Place a weight on top. Set in a baking pan to catch drippings, and refrigerate at least 1 hour.

To serve, carefully lift out of mold with the plastic sling and place on cutting board. Cut in half lengthwise, then cut crosswise in 1-inch-wide pieces. Serve on plates, allowing 2 pieces each. Top with dressing. Makes 6 to 7 servings, or 12 to 14 pieces.

Japanese pickles

In Japan, one of my favorite stalls in the covered market was the one that sold pickles. Your nose told you when you were approaching it. The odors drifting above the barrels and tubs of pickles dominated all others. As strong as these odors may seem to some people, we were not turned off by them.

We had developed a taste for pickles and a meal served without them seemed bland.

Vegetable pickles are served with almost every meal in Japan and are considered an aid to digestion. I like them for their zest—a nice contrast to plain boiled rice. The Chinese salt down vegetables as a way of preserving them, and use these vegetables primarily in cooking.

Of the many ways to prepare Japanese pickles, none produce the sour salty flavor of our dill pickles. The variety is limited only by what is in season.

You can buy pickles in Japanese markets. Since most of these are quick to prepare, you might want to try making them yourself. It's a way to really experience home-style cooking.

Pickles are usually served in small individual dishes, sliced or chopped. Two or three types are often combined in a single serving.

Takuan—Pickled Daikon

Your first smell of this pickle may stop you. Don't give up. Most people who get to the tasting stage become addicted.

4 quarts sliced peeled *daikon*,
 cut in finger-length spears
½ cup salt
1½ cups sugar
1 cup cider vinegar
2 cups water
¼ teaspoon monosodium glutamate
 Dried red chili peppers (optional)

1. Mix *daikon* and salt well and place in a large bowl or crock. Cover with a plate and weight down with a heavy object. Leave in a cool place overnight.

2. In the morning, drain off liquid and dry *daikon* with a clean dishtowel. Arrange in a single layer in baking pans and dry in the shade 4 hours. You can also use an electric fan indoors and dry for 2 hours.

3. Heat sugar, vinegar, water, and monosodium glutamate to boiling; cook for 3 minutes until sugar dissolves.

4. Pack *daikon* into hot sterilized jars, but not too tightly: the *daikon* will swell slightly as it ages. Add a chili pepper to each jar if desired. Pour boiling vinegar mixture over *daikon* and seal. Process in a boiling water bath for 20 minutes.

5. Allow to stand in a cool dark place at least 1 month before using. The color will change to a deep yellow. Makes 7 pints.

Quick Vinegared Daikon

2 pounds *daikon*
1 cup sugar
¼ cup white vinegar
1 cup water
¼ cup salt
Yellow food coloring

1. Peel *daikon* and thinly slice crosswise. Place in a quart jar or bowl.

2. Place sugar, vinegar, water, and salt in a saucepan; heat to boiling and cook just until sugar dissolves. Add a few drops food coloring to tint the syrup yellow. Cool.

3. Pour over *daikon*, cover, and refrigerate for 3 days before serving. Makes 3 cups.

Vegetables Pickled in Nuka

Nuka is rice bran used for curing many kinds of vegetables. The flavor of the *nuka* pickle is almost impossible to describe. It is mild, faintly sweet and salty, and very typically Japanese.

Once you start a batch of *nuka,* you can keep it going for a long time. Put small amounts of vegetables in the bran and they will be ready in a few days. As you eat the pickles, continue adding more fresh vegetables to cure. *Nuka* is available in Japanese food stores.

3 cups *nukazuke* (rice bran mixed with salt)
¼ cup *mirin*
2¼ cups fruit juice or syrup from any canned fruit
Vegetables (your choice)

1. Put rice bran in a dry frying pan and heat, stirring constantly, until it is lightly toasted. Turn bran into a glass, plastic, or earthenware container and mix with *mirin* and fruit juice.

2. Wash the vegetables, cut into chunks, and bury in the rice bran. You can pickle almost any vegetable, including peeled cucumbers, Japanese eggplant, *daikon,* turnips, cabbage, green peppers, asparagus, celery, and green tomatoes. Cover and refrigerate.

3. Cure for one or two days. Keep it going for as long as it lasts, stirring once each day. This lets in air and keeps it from fermenting. If you forget to stir and it turns sour, discard and start a new batch. Eventually the *nuka* becomes watery as the vegetables release liquid. Stir in more fresh *nuka* to keep mixture the consistency of oatmeal. Many people do not keep *nuka* in the refrigerator. I do it because it has a milder flavor.

To use, remove the vegetables from the bran, rinse with water, and squeeze out excess liquid. Chop or slice into thin pieces and serve with a sprinkling of soy sauce and monosodium glutamate.

Beer Dobu

This is similar to vegetables cured in *nuka* but is slightly sweeter. *Dobu* means "river ditch" or "wet dirt," an appropriate description of the curing mash.

1 can (12 oz.) beer
2 cups quick-cooking oatmeal
1½ cups brown sugar
5 tablespoons salt
Vegetables for pickling

1. Pour beer into a bowl and mix with oatmeal, brown sugar, and salt. Cover and let sit overnight in the refrigerator.

2. Cut up vegetables for pickling (for suggestions see recipe above) and bury in the *dobu.*

3. Cure for at least one day before rinsing off and eating. You can continue to add more vegetables to the *dobu,* but discard after two weeks. Stir once a day to let in air.

Eggplant Mustard Pickles

6 Japanese eggplant
¼ cup salt
2 teaspoons dry mustard
2 tablespoons *mirin*
1 tablespoon soy sauce

1. Cut unpeeled eggplant crosswise in 1-inch chunks. Add salt and mix well. Place in a bowl, cover with a plate, and weight down.

2. In the morning, drain liquid and pat eggplant dry with towel. Arrange in a single layer in a baking pan. Let dry (not in the sun) overnight.

3. Combine mustard, *mirin,* and soy sauce. Pour over eggplant and mix well. Pack into jars and leave in a cool place for 3 days. Cut into bite-size pieces before serving. Makes 2 pints.

Shio Zuke—Salt Pickles

This pickle is quite salty and is meant to be served with unseasoned rice.

1 medium cabbage or
1 head Chinese cabbage
2 tablespoons salt

1. Cut cabbage in 8 wedges; wash and drain. Place in a crock or deep bowl, sprinkling salt between the layers. Cover with a plate and top with a weight. Let stand at room temperature for 24 hours if using regular cabbage; 12 hours for Chinese cabbage.

2. With your hands, squeeze out liquid. If it is too salty for your taste, rinse with water first. Chop cabbage into small pieces and serve with soy sauce. Add a little lemon juice or grated ginger root if you wish.

A rock in a crock or a modern "pickle pot" can be used to keep salted vegetables submerged for Japanese pickles. In foreground, an assortment of vegetables cure in nuka.

Rice and noodles

To many Orientals, a meal without rice is like cornflakes without milk, and a day without noodles is like a week without Friday. Hot or cold, day in and day out, rice and noodles are the staples in Oriental kitchens. Here are instructions for cooking them and ways to serve them.

Most of my friends look forward to the appearance in supermarkets of seasonal treats like asparagus, corn on the cob, new potatoes. My Oriental friends anticipate also the appearance of newly harvested rice, which usually shows up in the fall.

It takes a dyed-in-the-wool rice-eater to appreciate fully the difference in flavor. I've finally caught it: a freshness that seems to burst forth from each grain—teasingly. A more obvious difference between the new and the old is the amount of water each requires for cooking. Because fresh rice has a higher moisture content, it requires less cooking water. Oriental cooks seem to make the adjustment by instinct. I am still practicing.

Use the right rice

The age of the rice makes far less difference to Oriental dishes than does the type of the rice and the way you cook it. The Chinese and Japanese use different types, employ different methods, and get noticeably different results. You should not use them interchangeably.

Although you might have your own opinion on this, neither the Chinese nor the Japanese salt their rice, on the grounds that a bland, unseasoned rice cleanses the palate and makes a better complement for gravies, sauces, pickles, and other accompaniments.

These basic instructions are for cooking rice on the stove. The same proportions apply if you use an automatic rice cooker—which I recommend. Cooking rice properly *is* a touchy business and takes practice. An automatic rice cooker eliminates timing guesswork, frees me to do other things, and keeps rice hot and moist until I'm ready to serve it. Nor do I fear that I'm slighting a culture by using one; many modern Oriental cooks swear by them.

Leftover rice

Cooked rice gets hard in the refrigerator. When I have only a little left over, I simply leave the pot out so anyone who passes by can help himself. However, if you have a lot, or plan to keep it for any length of time, it should be covered and refrigerated.

To use leftover rice, sprinkle over 2 tablespoons water, cover, and cook on low heat until heated through—or, with an automatic cooker, until it turns itself off. If you have a microwave oven, spoon rice on a plate, cover with clear plastic film, and heat for 3 to 5 minutes, depending upon the amount of rice.

Chinese Fried Rice

You can cook the Chinese-style rice for this dish a day ahead and chill it overnight in the refrigerator.

- **4 cups cold cooked rice**
- **2 teaspoons salad oil**
- **2 eggs, well beaten**
- **3 tablespoons salad oil**
- **1 cup cooked meat, shredded or diced (barbecued pork, ham, or chicken)**
- **1 tablespoon soy sauce**
- **1 tablespoon oyster sauce**
- **2 green onions and tops, finely chopped**
- **½ cup shredded lettuce (optional)**

1. Rub rice with your hands until all the grains are separated.

2. Heat the 2 teaspoons oil in a large frying pan. Pour in eggs and make a thin omelet. Remove from pan and cut into thin, short strips.

3. Heat the oil in a pan, add meat, and stir-fry until heated through. Add rice, stir lightly, and heat. Season with soy sauce and oyster sauce.

4. Sprinkle egg strips, green onions, and lettuce over the top; stir-fry 1 minute. Serves 4 to 6.

Korean Fried Rice

Make this version with Japanese-style rice. The rice grains will not be completely separated, even if you chill the rice overnight, so you can make it without advance planning. Let the freshly cooked rice stand for 30

Chinese-style Rice

The Chinese prefer a long-kernel rice that cooks up fluffy and dry, with each grain separate. The dry, flat Texas Patna is the most readily available long-grain rice throughout the U.S.

Measure 1 cup rice into a heavy pan. To remove dust, cover with cold water; drain. Add 1½ cups cold water (up to 1¾ cups if you prefer it softer). Stirring occasionally to prevent sticking, boil *uncovered* over medium high heat until most of the water is absorbed; craterlike holes will form on the surface. Turn heat to low, cover, and steam until rice is soft, 20 to 25 minutes. Makes 2 cups.

minutes after steaming before using it.

I like this dish because it eats up odds and ends of vegetables—a stalk of celery, a piece of green pepper, a wedge of cabbage can go in instead of or in addition to those called for. The trick in ad-libbing with tidbits is to cut them in thin slices and add them according to their water content: the firm, longer-cooking ones first, the thin, quick-cooking ones last.

- **2 teaspoons sesame seeds**
- **½ pound boneless beef (chuck roast or top round), cut in thin strips**
- **2 tablespoons soy sauce**
- **½ teaspoon salt**
- **½ teaspoon sugar**
- **1 clove garlic, minced**
- **3 green onions and tops, finely chopped**
- **4 tablespoons salad oil**
- **2 small carrots, thinly sliced crosswise**
- **6 fresh mushrooms, thinly sliced**
- **15 edible podded peas, ends and side strings removed, cut in bite-size pieces**
- **½ pound bean sprouts, washed and drained**
- **4 cups cooked Japanese-style rice**

1. Place sesame seeds in a small pan and toast over medium-low heat until the seeds brown lightly and begin to jump in the pan. Remove from pan at once (if you don't they will continue to cook), cool slightly. Crush seeds, using a mortar and pestle or sesame seed grinder.

2. Marinate meat with soy sauce, salt, sugar, sesame seeds, garlic, and green onions for 1 hour.

3. Heat 2 tablespoons of the oil in a large frying pan. When very hot, add meat and spread in a thin layer. Cook for 30 seconds, turn to brown other side for 30 seconds, and remove from pan. Unlike most stir-frying, this meat should not be stirred continuously or it will get juicy from the marinade and simmer instead of fry.

4. Heat the remaining 2 tablespoons oil in pan. Add carrots and stir-fry over high heat for 2 minutes. Toss in mushrooms and stir-fry 2 more minutes. Add peas and bean sprouts and stir-fry 1 minute. Return meat to pan.

5. Turn off heat and add rice. Break up rice with a spoon and combine with meat and vegetables. Taste. If you cooked the rice plain, you may want to add salt. Serves 4 to 6.

Oyako Donburi—Rice with Chicken and Egg

Japanese *donburi,* a favorite lunch-time snack, is hot rice served with various toppings. It derives its name from the *donburi* (big bowl) in which it is served.

- **¼ cup *sake***
- **⅓ cup soy sauce**
- **⅓ cup sugar**
- **3 tablespoons *mirin***
- **1 cup water**
- **½ pound boned chicken, cut in ½-inch cubes**
- **4 dried mushrooms, presoaked and thinly sliced**
- **3 green onions and tops, cut diagonally in 1½-inch lengths**
- **4 eggs, well-beaten**
- **4 cups hot cooked rice**

1. Place *sake,* soy sauce, sugar, *mirin,* and water in a saucepan and heat just to boiling point. Add chicken and mushrooms and simmer 5 minutes. Add green onions and cook 1 minute.

2. Pour in eggs all at once. When mixture begins to bubble around the edges of the pan, turn down heat and cover. Cook for 3 minutes or until the eggs look scrambled. To avoid scorching, stir several times after eggs have been added.

3. Serve rice in 4 bowls and ladle egg-and-soup mixture over rice. Serves 4.

Donburi in a Hurry

This is one of the simplest *donburi* devised. Very good when you're short on time.

- **1 can (7 oz.) tuna fish**
- **¼ cup mayonnaise**
- **1 tablespoon soy sauce**
- **1 stalk celery, finely chopped**

Drain the oil from the can of tuna. Break up with a fork and mix with mayonnaise, soy sauce, and celery. Serve cold over hot cooked rice and serve with *takuan* (pickled *daikon*). (See page 42.)

Japanese-style Rice

The Japanese like a shorter-grained rice that cooks up moist and rather sticky (much easier for the beginner to handle with chopsticks). Look for these labels: Kokuho, Calrose, Lucky Rose, Blue Rose, Japan Rose, Nato, Magnolia, and Zenith.

Short and medium-grained rice is coated with talc, so be sure to wash it well. (There is no direct loss of nutrients.) Place rice in a heavy pan; cover with water; rub rice between your palms; drain. Continue dousing, rubbing, and draining until the water runs clear.

Once you've started cooking it, *keep your hands off the lid.*

To 1 cup rice, add 1 cup of water. Cover pan and let soak—for about an hour, if you have time. Bring rice to a boil quickly over high heat. *Don't lift the lid; listen.* Reduce heat to low and simmer for 20 minutes. *Without lifting the lid,* turn off heat and let stand 5 to 10 minutes. Fold rice over once—carefully—to fluff up the kernels. Makes 2 cups rice.

Japanese noodles

Until we lived in Japan, the only Oriental noodle I saw with regularity was the *chow mein* noodle. Our first experience with bowls of steaming *soba* (buckwheat noodles in rich broth) came early, and we delighted in exploring the neighborhood *soba* shops. The customary way of eating it entranced our children and appealed to the child in us: you just pick up the bowl and slurp.

The Japanese eat a great variety of noodles—thick white *udon,* thinner *soba,* (some tan, some flavored with green tea), thinnest *somen*—in a great variety of situations. They are a quick snack to eat at the train station, on the ski slopes, at shrine festivities (where they are sold from small stands), or a fast meal in a restaurant or at home. (Each cook varies them; it's hard to find the same one twice.)

Noodle broth

When a Japanese cook wants noodles in broth, she does not make it as you might make noodle soup: by dropping a handful or two of noodles into a pan of simmering soup for the last few minutes of cooking. She cooks the noodles in clear water, pours off the cooking water, distributes the noodles in serving bowls, then pours hot broth over them.

Japanese hardware stores and some kitchen specialty shops sell a basket designed especially for dipping noodles. It is 4 inches in diameter and about 5 inches high with a vertical handle. It is not essential to good noodle-cooking but is a handsome piece of equipment and provides an efficient way to drain and reheat individual servings. To reheat, you hang it (filled) over the rim of a boiling kettle of water by means of a clip attached to the basket.

Instant noodles

Precooked noodles are handy in an emergency and are available everywhere. Their seasonings are basically Japanese, though many are Chinese-type. They cook in a couple of minutes and jazz up nicely with fresh garnishes (chopped green onion, thinly sliced Chinese cabbage, a few green peas) or with slivers of cooked meat. There are several kinds, under several labels: *ramen, saimin* (a Hawaiian version), *yaki soba, chuka soba,* hen's egg noodles, and imitation noodles. (Imitation noodles really are noodles but they contain no egg. This wording is used to satisfy American government labeling requirements.) Cooking instructions are on their packages.

You can assemble individual casseroles of Nabeyaki Udon ahead of time. Pour over broth before baking.

Nabeyaki Udon

You can make this with egg instead of prawns and *kamaboko*. Drop 1 egg in each bowl, along with the other garnishes, cover, and bake until egg is set.

16 spinach leaves and stems
½ pound dried *udon* noodles cooked according to directions below
½ chicken breast, skinned, boned, and cut in 8 bite-size pieces
2 fresh mushrooms, sliced
4 slices *kamaboko* (fish cake)

4 cups noodle broth
2 green onions and tops, cut in 1½-inch lengths
8 cooked prawns, shelled
Japanese pepper-spice

1. Cook spinach in boiling water for 1 minute, drain, and rinse with cold water. Arrange leaves and stems parallel in a bundle; gently squeeze out the water; cut in 1-inch lengths.

2. Divide noodles among 4 individual casseroles or place in one casserole. Divide the garnishes so each casserole has some of the chicken, mushrooms, and *kamaboko*. Add heated soup broth.

3. Cover and bake in a moderate oven (350°) for 15 minutes. Arrange spinach, green onions, and prawns over noodles. Re-cover and continue baking 5 more minutes. Serve with chopsticks or a fork and a spoon. The Japanese pepper-spice can be sprinkled over top, if desired. Serves 4.

Soba—Buckwheat Noodles

2 pieces fried soybean cake (*aburage*)
½ cup *dashi* or chicken stock
2 tablespoons soy sauce
2 teaspoons sugar
1 tablespoon *mirin*
Dash of monosodium glutamate
½ chicken breast, skinned, boned, and cut in 8 bite-size pieces
4 thin slices bamboo shoots
2 dried mushrooms, presoaked and sliced in ¼-inch widths
4 cups noodle broth
3 green onions, sliced diagonally in 1½-inch lengths
¾ pound dried *soba* noodles, cooked or reheated according to directions at left.

1. Dip fried bean cake in boiling water to remove excess oil, then slice in ½-inch widths. Place in a saucepan with *dashi* or chicken stock, soy sauce, sugar, *mirin,* monosodium glutamate, chicken, bamboo shoots, and mushrooms. Simmer until most of the liquid has been absorbed, about 7 minutes.

2. Heat soup broth for noodles. Add green onion and cook for 30 seconds.

3. Divide heated noodles in 4 bowls. Arrange bean cake, chicken, bamboo shoots, mushrooms, and green onions on top of *soba* and pour hot broth over all. Serves 4.

To Cook Japanese Noodles

All dried noodles (not the instant ones) are prepared in the same way.

Heat a large kettle of water to boiling. Add noodles, stirring several times to separate. When the water comes to a full boil, add ½ cup cold water. Bring to a boil; add another ½ cup cold water. Continue cooking until noodles are tender.

Somen:	3 to 4 minutes
Soba:	6 to 7 minutes
Udon:	12 to 15 minutes

Be careful not to overcook. Start the timing when the noodles go into the water.

Pour into a colander; rinse with cold water. Use immediately, or refrigerate in a covered container for a day or two. Reheat by dipping in hot water.

To Make Japanese Noodle Broth

Japanese noodles are very bland, so it is important to serve them in a flavorful broth. *Dashi* is a favorite with the Japanese. I often use chicken broth—when I'm in a hurry, or when authenticity is not the point. (But don't use pork broth unless you don't mind giving Japanese noodles a Chinese flavor.)

Here is another delicious broth. It is the backbone of most of the recipes that follow, and serves well over boiled noodles of any kind.

4 cups *dashi* (page 33) or chicken stock
⅓ cup soy sauce
⅓ cup *mirin* or dry sherry
½ teaspoon sugar
Dash *each* salt and monosodium glutamate

Mix all ingredients together in pan. Bring to boil; simmer for 30 seconds. Use immediately, or keep refrigerated for up to two days. Plan on 1 to 1¼ cups broth for each serving of noodles.

Tomato Beef is delicious alone, but even better over pan-fried noodles.

Teruko's Summer Somen

My friend, Teruko, introduced me to cold noodles on a humid, sticky day. But refreshing, rather than sticky, is the word to describe her summer specialty.

I have never eaten this with a fork and I think it would be difficult. When you use *hashi* (chopsticks), you pick up the *somen* and let water from ice cubes drain so the noodles won't dilute the dipping sauce.

1 cup *dashi* or chicken stock
¼ cup *mirin*
⅓ cup soy sauce
1 tablespoon sugar
Dash of monosodium glutamate
12 prawns, shelled and deveined
1 small Japanese cucumber or ⅓ large thin-skinned cucumber
¾ pound dried *somen*, cooked and chilled
¼ cup canned *ginkgo* nuts
½ pound *tofu* (soybean cake), cut in 1½-inch cubes
3 green onions and tops, finely chopped

1. To prepare dipping sauce, mix *dashi, mirin,* soy sauce, sugar, and monosodium glutamate in a saucepan and simmer for 4 minutes; chill.

2. Cook prawns in boiling salted water for 3 minutes; drain and chill. Thinly slice unpeeled cucumber.

3. Arrange chilled, cooked *somen* in 4 bowls. Place several ice cubes in each bowl on top of the *somen.* Garnish each serving with prawns, cucumbers, *ginkgo* nuts, and *tofu.* Divide dipping sauce into 4 other small bowls or Japanese tea cups. Place green onions on a small plate.

4. Each person adds green onions to his dipping sauce, then dips the *somen* and garnishes in the sauce. Serves 4.

Chinese noodles

Chinese noodles, called *mein,* are available in both the fresh and dried form. The most common variety looks like spaghetti, only thinner. Follow the same cooking directions described under Japanese noodles (see page 47); cook the dried noodles 7 to 10 minutes, the fresh ones 2 to 3 minutes. Serve the noodles in bowls with hot chicken or pork broth and garnish with sliced barbecued pork or slivers of cooked chicken meat, shredded green onion, parboiled edible podded peas or *bok choy,* and Chinese parsley.

To prepare *chow mein* with Cantonese-style pan-fried noodles, I've used the dried noodles, but prefer the fresh Chinese-style egg noodles. When you market, buy several bags. They freeze well.

Most Chinese cooks use a wok to fry the noodles into a sheet. But after much experimenting I've found it easier to fry them in a flat-bottom nonstick frying pan. This method requires less cooking oil and makes less splatter. The noodles come out golden brown and crisp on the outside, soft on the inside.

Tomato Beef Chow Mein

To add even more contrast of flavor, serve this with little dishes of soy, vinegar, and mustard.

½ flank steak (about ¾ pound), cut in strips ⅛ inch wide and 1½ inches long

Marinade:
2 teaspoons cornstarch
1 tablespoon soy sauce
1 teaspoon sherry
½ teaspoon salt
⅛ teaspoon monosodium glutamate
1 clove garlic, minced

2 quarts water
1 pound fresh Chinese-style egg noodles
2 tablespoons soy sauce
Salad oil for frying

Gravy:
1 tablespoon *each* soy sauce, Worcestershire, and cornstarch
3 tablespoons catsup
1 teaspoon curry powder
½ cup water

4 tablespoons oil
Salt
2 large stalks celery, sliced diagonally ⅛ inch thick
1 medium onion, cut in wedges; separate layers
1 green pepper, cut in bite-size pieces
3 medium tomatoes, cut in 6 wedges each

1. Marinate meat in mixture of cornstarch, soy sauce, sherry, salt, monosodium glutamate, and garlic. Set aside while you prepare noodles and vegetables.

2. Heat 2 quarts water to boiling. Add noodles, stir, and again bring to a boil. Add ½ cup cold water, reduce heat, and simmer 2 to 3 minutes. Drain, rinse with cold water, and toss noodles with the 2 tablespoons soy sauce.

3. Heat 2 tablespoons salad oil in a nonstick frying pan. Spread one-third of noodles in pan and cook, without stirring, over high heat until light brown. Drizzle a few drops oil around the edges of the noodles if they appear to be sticking. Turn the sheet of noodles to brown other side. Repeat with remaining noodles, adding oil as needed. Keep warm.

4. Prepare gravy by combining the soy sauce, Worcestershire, cornstarch, catsup, curry powder, and water.

5. Heat 2 tablespoons of the oil in a wok or large frying pan. Sprinkle a little salt over the oil, then stir-fry celery and onion 2 minutes. Add green pepper and cook 1 minute. Add tomatoes and heat through. Remove from pan.

6. Heat the remaining 2 tablespoons oil in wok and stir-fry marinated meat for 1 minute or until just browned on the outside. Add vegetables to meat. Stir gravy to recombine ingredients; pour over meat and vegetables, stir and cook until sauce thickens. Stack pan-fried noodles on a platter and cover with meat sauce. Serves 4 to 6.

Note: To make serving easier, cut the fried noodles into smaller portions, or you can fry individual servings of noodles in a 6-inch frying pan.

Cellophane noodles

Looking for all the world like fragile skeins of transparent wire, these noodles are made from dried mung beans. They're sold under many names: bean threads, transparent noodles, long rice, *fun see, sai fun,* and *harusame.* Don't confuse them with *shirataki,* a pungent Japanese noodle made of yam bean threads.

Although they have no flavor of their own, cellophane noodles absorb the flavors of cooking liquids. And they have texture a-plenty—a chewiness and springiness that no other noodle offers.

It is almost impossible to pull the bundles apart. Cut off the amount you need with scissors, and soak in hot water for 30 minutes. This softens them so you can cut them into shorter

lengths and prepares them for quick cooking.

Here's one good way to serve them. Enthusiasts use them as a base for almost any stir-fried combination. Remember that they depend upon a seasoned broth for flavor, and note that they take only 3 minutes to cook.

Cellophane Noodles with Pork

20 edible podded peas, ends and side strings removed
½ cup chicken stock
3 tablespoons soy sauce
¼ pound boneless pork, cut in matchstick-size pieces
1 teaspoon *each* cornstarch and soy sauce
3 tablespoons salad oil
4 dried mushrooms, presoaked and thinly sliced
¼ pound (4 oz.) cellophane noodles, presoaked 30 minutes, then cut in 3-inch lengths
2 green onions and tops, cut in 1½-inch lengths and slivered
Few sprigs Chinese parsley

1. Cut peas lengthwise in thin slivers. Cook in boiling salted water 2 minutes; drain and rinse with cold water. Combine chicken stock and soy sauce; reserve.

2. Coat meat with a mixture of the cornstarch and soy sauce.

3. Heat oil in a wok or large frying pan. Add meat and stir-fry for 4 minutes. Add mushrooms and continue cooking 3 minutes.

4. Add cellophane noodles to pan and stir lightly. Pour in half the chicken-stock mixture. Cover and cook for 3 minutes, stirring occasionally. Add remaining chicken-stock mixture and cook just until liquid is absorbed.

5. Transfer to a serving bowl and garnish with slivered peas, green onions, and Chinese parsley. Serves 4.

Most people like cellophane noodles the first time—with chopsticks or with a fork.

Rice sticks

When you buy them in a package, *mai fun* (vermicelli made from rice) are hard to tell from cellophane noodles. When you fry them in deep fat, they instantly puff up and become crisp, and look and taste like no noodle you ever saw.

If the heat is too high, they will burn. If the heat is too low, they will stew rather than sizzle. Keep in mind that each batch is worth only two or three cents and keep trying. By the third time you'll be able to judge the heat and you can pat yourself on the back for persistence.

Cook them a skimpy handful at a time, in hot, deep fat (350°). As soon as they are puffy and crisp, remove and drain. You can store them for several weeks in a tightly covered can, or use them immediately in Chinese Chicken Salad (page 41). For a crunchy snack, sprinkle them lightly with salt while they're still hot.

1. Fried rice sticks: Heat 2 inches oil in wok. Add small handful rice sticks.

2. Presto! They instantly puff up, become crisp, and turn a pale straw color.

3. Remove from wok; drain. Serve in salad or as a crisp topping for vegetables.

Sushi

Whoever called *sushi* "the Japanese sandwich" was not describing its appearance or comparing its ingredients or explaining its assembly. He was pointing out the cultural parallels: their prevalence, popularity, and round-the-clock welcome. As the sandwich in America, *sushi* in Japan is an after-school snack, a shopper's pick-up, a hot-beverage accompaniment, a lunch, a dinner, a canapé, a late-evening spread. Depending on the variety, it can be moderately priced or outrageously expensive. It goes to picnics, parks, and parties.

More than a sandwich

Basically, *sushi* is vinegared rice—but that alone is no more *sushi* than bread alone is a sandwich. It's the additions that count: the fish, shellfish, pickles, and vegetables that go in, on, or around the rice as fillings, toppings, and wrappings.

And here the parallels end. You cannot slap *sushi* together on impulse in a couple of minutes. In Japan, *sushi* is a "convenience" food only in the sense that it is readily available in shops, bars, and restaurants. Because it is so omnipresent, and so good ready-made (it takes years of apprenticeship to become a professional *sushi* maker), most housewives in Japan probably buy it rather than make it. I know I did. But by the time we came home again my whole family had developed a taste for it, so I had to start plumbing its mysteries.

I don't want to exaggerate its difficulties. Even an amateur can get it together on the first try.

Fan sushi rice (you can use a newspaper) as you fold in the seasoned vinegar. This cools the rice quickly and brings out the luster of the grain.

Oshi-zushi: Lay marinated mackerel fillet over sushi rice in wooden mold.

Replace mold cover and press down so the fish and rice "sandwich" together.

Remove sides of mold and top cover. Rub seasoned vinegar over the knife blade.

Four basic forms

Sushi can be made four different ways: pressed, hand-shaped, bagged, and rolled.

Many Westerners who first see or taste rolled *sushi* are turned off by the discovery that its wrapper is seaweed. I've always enjoyed seaweed, considering it just another vegetable that happens to grow in seawater instead of soil (carrots) or fresh water (water chestnuts). But only the rolled *sushi* is in seaweed, and if seaweed is not your bag you can wrap it in ham or an omelet.

Sushi is always served at room temperature, and tastes best when eaten the day it is made. It is very perishable; cover leftovers tightly and refrigerate. The kernels will get a little hard, but the flavors will be good for a day or two.

Be smart. Serve your first batch to your family and neighbors, who won't judge it with an experienced eye, rather than to visiting Japanese, who will. The first time I made it, under the tutelage of a Japanese friend, the rolls bulged at one end, sagged at the other, and oozed with the excess vinegar I'd slathered on my hands to keep the rice from sticking. But my long-suffering neighbors enjoyed it, my family was proud of my attempt, and I felt just successful enough to want to try again.

After you've mastered the basic structure, you needn't be afraid to experiment on your own.

Pressed sushi

The Japanese use a special wooden mold called *oshiwaku.* (See the illustration on page 53 for construction details.) In Japan the name changes with each topping. All we could be sure of was that if we asked for "Osaka-style" we would get pressed *sushi.*

Oshi-zushi—Pressed Sushi

This includes mackerel *(saba)* that has "cooked" in a marinade for several days.

1½ pound mackerel
2 tablespoons salt

Marinade:
¾ cup lemon juice
2 tablespoons white vinegar
3 tablespoons sugar
1 teaspoon salt
½ teaspoon monosodium glutamate
1 teaspoon grated ginger root
6 cups *sushi* rice (cooked)
2 teaspoons *wasabi*
  (Japanese horseradish)

Clean 1½ pound mackerel (fresh or frozen); cut off head and tail. Split in half lengthwise to get two fillets. Remove large bones. Rub all over with salt. Let stand overnight in the refrigerator.

In the morning, pull off the clear film from the skin and remove remaining bones. (The salting expedites this.) Prepare a marinade by combining lemon juice, white vinegar, sugar, salt, monosodium glutamate, and ginger root. Pour over fish and refrigerate, covered, for from 1 to 4 days.

Prepare 6 cups *sushi* rice (cooked) on the day you serve it. In a small bowl, mix *wasabi* with a little water—to get the consistency of sour cream. (The Japanese say that the more fiery the temperament of the cook, the hotter the taste of *wasabi.)*

To assemble: Brush a thin layer of vinegar mixture over the bottom of the mold. Pack *sushi* rice in to ¾-inch deep, pressing evenly with your fingertips. Spread with *thin* film of *wasabi.* Cut one mackerel fillet to fit the mold; place on top. Replace mold cover and press down firmly.

Remove cover and sides. Rub a little vinegar mixture over a sharp knife, and cut into serving pieces. Transfer *sushi* to a tray, and repeat assembly with the second fillet.

Rice for Sushi

3 cups Japanese-style rice
3¼ cups water
¾ cup white vinegar
⅓ cup plus 2 tablespoons sugar
2 tablespoons salt
2 teaspoons monosodium glutamate

Cook rice with 3¼ cups water. Follow method on page 46. In a saucepan cook vinegar, sugar, salt, and monosodium glutamate until sugar dissolves; cool.

Using a rice paddle, scoop cooked rice into a large, shallow baking pan. Pour half the vinegar mixture evenly over the surface; fold liquid in—carefully, without mashing kernels. At the same time, fan the rice. This "fanning" brings out the luster of the grain. Continue fanning and folding until little liquid is left. The rice absorbs the excess liquid as it cools. Makes 6 cups *sushi* rice.

Use the remaining vinegar mixture as you assemble the *sushi.* Dip your fingertips into it to keep the rice from sticking to your fingertips.

Cut sushi *in finger-length pieces. Save the corners for the non-fish eaters.*

Serve as first course or hors d'oeuvre. Try other fish, shellfish for toppings.

Hosomaki: Lay nori on bamboo mat; cover with sushi rice and thin film of wasabi.

Lay cucumber, takuan, or fish strip on rice. Lift mat to help roll into cylinder.

Roll up like jelly roll. Press mat around rolled sushi to seal the edges.

Hand-shaped sushi

These are the quickest to make, and adapt to assemble-your-own family meals or to run-the-gamut "canapé" trays.

Nigiri-zushi

Sometimes called "Tokyo-style," this *is* a style rather than a recipe. You can top it with raw tuna, sea bass, abalone, octopus, squid, scallops . . . or with prawns that you've parboiled and butterflied.

To assemble each one, shape about 2 tablespoons *sushi* rice into a 1 by 2-inch "finger." Top with a dab of *wasabi* paste and a custom-cut piece of the fish of your choice, draping it prettily over the sides and ends.

You can make another hand-shaped *sushi* to resemble *temari,* a hand ball Japanese children play with. Shape *sushi* rice into a 1-inch ball.. Drape thin strips of omelet and par-boiled strips of carrot and edible podded peas over the ball. Press a thin band of *nori* around the diameter of the ball to hold the vegetables in place. (See photo of *sushi* tray.)

Bagged sushi

The little bags made of fried bean cake and filled with *sushi* rice and vege-

Stuff sushi rice flavored with chicken, vegetables into bags of fried bean cake.

tables are sometimes called *kitsune-zushi* because their color resembles the fox *(kitsune).* They are a favorite picnic food.

Age—zushi

6 pieces *aburage* (fried soybean cake)
1 cup chicken stock
1 tablespoon soy sauce
2 tablespoons sugar
Monosodium glutamate
½ chicken breast, skinned, boned, and cut in ¼-inch squares
2 dried mushrooms, presoaked and diced
6 edible-pod peas
¼ cup diced omelet
3 cups prepared *sushi* rice

Cut bean cake squares in half and gently pull open the center of each, making little bags. Simmer in water to cover, 20 minutes. Drain.

Place chicken stock, soy sauce, sugar, and a dash of monosodium glutamate in a saucepan. Bring to a boil; add the bags and simmer 15 minutes. Carefully spoon out bags; drain. Cook chicken breasts in remaining liquid for about 5 minutes. Remove. Add mushrooms to pan and cook for 15 minutes. If most of the liquid is gone add ⅓ cup chicken stock, 1 teaspoon each soy sauce and sugar, and a dash of monosodium

It's a special day to come home from school and find a tray of age-zushi.

glutamate. Drain mushrooms when tender. Snap ends off peas; pull side strings. Cut into small pieces. Parboil in salted water 1 minute. Drain and rinse with cold water. Gently combine chicken, vegetables, omelet, and *sushi* rice. Fill bags; roll over top to close. Makes 12.

Hosomaki—small roll

In this *sushi,* the rice is spread on a wrapping, it is filled with any one of various goodies, rolled up, and sliced into rounds.

The usual wrapping is *nori* (laver seaweed); the best of the seaweeds is *yaki-nori* which is a very dark green. If you don't want to use *nori* as a wrapper use thin slices of boiled ham or thin sheets of omelet as wrappers. (To prepare an omelet wrapper, beat together 6 eggs, 1 tablespoon sugar, ½ teaspoon salt, and a dash of monosodium glutamate. Cook in thin layers in a lightly greased pan.) If you use *nori,* make each sheet 4 inches by 7 inches. (See photos above.) Use any of the following ingredients as a filling.

✓Takuan (pickled *daikon*). Cut in thin strips 7 inches long. Sprinkle toasted sesame seeds between the rice and *takuan.*

✓Striped bass or tuna. Cut raw bone-less fish into thin strips. Spread a thin film of *wasabi* paste on rice when using fish filling.

✓Cucumbers. Peel and cut into thin strips, 7 inches long. Sprinkle with salt; let stand 15 minutes. Squeeze out liquid. Spread a film of *wasabi* paste on rice when using cucumber.

Norimaki—large roll

This is assembled the same way as *hosomaki* except each roll is larger and contains five ingredients instead of one. The size of the *nori* sheets is 7 by 8 inches, twice the size of *hosomaki.* To make the filling for *norimaki,* prepare the following five ingredients:

✔*Kampyo* (dried gourd strips). Cut 8 pieces, 7 inches in length. Parboil in water to cover for 20 minutes, drain, and rinse. Place in a pan with ½ cup *dashi* or water, 3 tablespoons soy sauce, 1 tablespoon sugar and 1 tablespoon *mirin.* Simmer for 20 minutes.

✔Dried mushrooms. Presoak 4 large or 6 small mushrooms for 20 minutes. Squeeze out excess water and cut in thin strips. Cook in a pan with ½ cup *dashi,* 3 tablespoons soy sauce, 1 tablespoon sugar, and 1 tablespoon *mirin* for 20 minutes. The mushrooms are not cooked with the *kampyo* be-

cause each item should retain its own flavor.

✔*Kamaboko* (fish cake). Cut into thin strips.

✔Spinach. Wash I bunch spinach, then boil briefly in boiling salted water for 2 minutes. Drain and rinse in cold water. Arrange spinach so all the leaves and stems are parallel and gently squeeze out water. Cut ¼-inch thick bundles in 7-inch lengths.

✔Omelet. Beat 2 eggs with a pinch of salt, and 1 teaspoon sugar and fry into a thin omelet. Cut into thin strips.

Norimaki: Five different ingredients make a colorful filling in this sushi.

Make your own sushi press

Quite simple to make out of almost any wood. The one shown in the photos is made of pine, but most hardwoods would work just as well.

All wood is ½ inch thick. Inside dimensions of the press shown are 4″ x 8″ x 1½″, but they're not critical as long as the top and bottom fit just loosely into the box.

Cross braces keep top and bottom from warping. Cut those on top flush with sides.

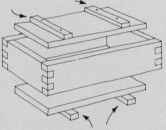

Let cross braces on bottom extend ½ inch so it does *not* slide into the box.

To make corners strong the Japanese dove-tail and glue them. Here are three other ways without special tools:

HINGES OR METAL CORNERS. Plain or decorative ones are available or you can cut your own from brass stock or soup cans with tin snips.

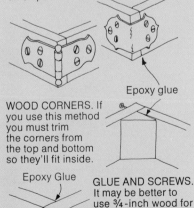

Epoxy glue

WOOD CORNERS. If you use this method you must trim the corners from the top and bottom so they'll fit inside.

Epoxy Glue

GLUE AND SCREWS. It may be better to use ¾-inch wood for the box to give the glue more holding surface.

Sushi party: There are wrappings, fillings, toppings to please all tastes. Provide soy sauce for dipping sauce.

Ways with vegetables

**Don't be afraid to experiment with vegetables.
Although each one is a little different,
their basic cooking is reduced to a single rule:
Cook as fast as you can,
and serve immediately.**

One of the earliest pleasures when you start adventuring in Oriental foods is widening your vegetable horizons. Japanese and Chinese markets are full of mysterious and challenging vegetables, and supermarkets are stocking a wider variety each year.

If you're even more adventuresome you can grow your own. Turn to the chapter on growing Oriental vegetables (page 80); many of these will probably be new to you since they seldom show up in American markets.

Whether you cook a favorite vegetable or experiment with a new one, one of the first things to learn is that Oriental-style vegetables should look as fresh and colorful after cooking as they do before. This is especially true when vegetables are parboiled and served bright, crisp, and cold (see chapter on salads, page 38). This is equally true when they are stir-fried and served bright, crisp, and hot. Many Americans might say this isn't as much a matter of learning to *cook* vegetables as it is a matter of learning to *undercook* them. However you approach it, the stir-fry technique is one you must master if you want to bring the true flavor of the Orient to your table.

Timing vegetables

You can stir-fry dozens of vegetables, but it isn't necessary to have a separate recipe for each one. What you need to know is that each vegetable has its own cooking time because of differences in texture and water content. Bean sprouts, for example, release their own juices and will cook in one minute, while a firm vegetable like broccoli may take 4 to

⬦
Only the freshest vegetables go into a shopper's basket in Chinatown.

5 minutes to cook and need a little water to become tender. The way you cut a vegetable also affects the cooking time; wedges naturally take longer than shreds. Also, remember that the fresher the vegetable, the shorter the cooking time.

Rules for stir-frying

A basic recipe for stir-frying is below. Here are some extra tips to help make stir-frying become a natural kitchen skill for you.

Assemble everything ahead. Cut vegetables, line up seasonings, and mix gravy before you start to cook. Stir-frying is so fast, you need to give it your full attention.

Cut in the same shape. Cut all the vegetables for one dish in the same size. Match wedges with wedges, shreds with shreds, cubes with cubes. This is so the vegetables will cook in the same amount of time, and it gives a pleasing appearance to the finished dish.

Separate by cooking times. Stir-fry vegetables individually when combining those with different cooking times. Set each cooked vegetable aside, then toss the combination together before serving. Or, add the firmest vegetables to the pan first, the most tender ones last.

Cook in a very hot wok. Heat the empty wok, then heat oil to sizzling, swirl about in the pan, then add the vegetables. If you add vegetables to a cold pan or to cold oil, they will be limp and soggy.

Don't overcrowd the pan. This reduces the heat of the wok and you'll wind up with stewed vegetables instead of stir-fried ones.

Don't mix many types of vegetables. Limit combination to three or four kinds of vegetables unless you are *purposely* trying to get rid of leftovers. A color contrast is desirable but too many bits and pieces add up to a hodgepodge.

Basic Stir-Fried Vegetables

2 tablespoons salad oil
½ teaspoon salt
2 thin slices ginger root, minced
1 clove garlic, peeled and minced
1 pound cut vegetables
½ teaspoon sugar
 Water (optional)
 Gravy: 1 tablespoon cornstarch mixed with 2 teaspoons soy sauce and
 ½ cup chicken stock or water (optional)

Heat wok. Add oil and heat. Add salt, ginger, garlic, and vegetables. Stir-fry around wok 1 minute to coat with oil. Adjust heat to prevent scorching.

Add sugar. If you are cooking soft vegetables, stop cooking at this time. For firmer vegetables, add 1 to 2 tablespoons water, cover, and cook for 2 minutes or until crisp tender. If vegetables are not quite done, cook another minute or two, adding another tablespoon or so of water if wok is dry.

Serve at once, or if you wish a gravy, stir gravy mixture to recombine it; pour over vegetables, and stir and cook for 30 seconds or until sauce thickens. Serves 4.

The art of cutting and slicing

There are no hard and fast rules for cutting vegetables. Their own nature and how you use them determines the shape.

Clockwise from top left. Carrots can be cut many ways. Split in half lengthwise and thinly slice, or quarter lengthwise and thinly slice. To cut in matchstick pieces, cut in 3-inch lengths. Cut a thin slice from the rounded side so the carrot will lie flat; slice through carrot making slices ⅛ inch thick. Lay slices flat and cut in matchstick pieces. For the mixed-shape pieces of carrot, cut crosswise at a 45° angle, reversing the knife blade with each cut. To make a diagonal cut, use tip of cleaver as a pivot, and slice through carrot at an angle.

The asparagus is cut with a diagonal cut and a roll-cut. To roll-cut, make a diagonal slice straight down, roll asparagus one-quarter turn, and slice again.

The shape of canned bamboo shoots (below asparagus) determines cut.

Celery is cut diagonally in two ways. For the top half the knife blade is held at a 45° angle over the celery and each piece is shaved off. Bottom half shows diagonal cut.

Center section of Oriental cucumber is strip peeled. The green skin is left for color. The larger cucumber is cut in rounds, half rounds, and quarter rounds with seeds removed.

Daikon (Japanese radish) in upper right is cut in thick and thin slices. Slices can be halved, quartered, or trimmed and cut in squares or cubes. Shredded *daikon* was cut with fine shredder blade of Japanese cutter.

Turnip on small cutting board is used for decorative garnish. Make checkerboard cuts ⅛ inch apart, cutting down so knife blade stops when it hits chopsticks.

Onion is cut in half lengthwise, then cut crosswise. Chinese cooks generally separate layers, Japanese cooks keep each slice intact.

For general cooking, cut mushrooms lengthwise through the stem.

On the large cutting board, a fan cut is a dramatic way to cut Oriental eggplant for barbecuing or baking. Zucchini or yellow summer squash look appealing this way too.

Vegetables with meat

When combining meat with vegetables, use flank steak or pork butt; slice across the grain in thin strips. Use roughly one part meat to four parts vegetables. Marinate ¼ pound meat for 15 minutes in 1 teaspoon cornstarch, 1 teaspoon sherry, 1 teaspoon soy sauce, and ½ teaspoon salt. Heat 2 tablespoons oil in wok; add meat and stir-fry beef for 1½ minutes. Cook pork for 5 minutes or until no longer pink. Remove meat from pan. Cook vegetables (see basic recipe). When crisp tender, return meat to pan, pour in gravy, and cook until thickened.

With cooked meat. Follow the recipe for basic stir-fried vegetables. Thirty seconds before vegetables are done, add thin slices of barbecued pork, roast pork, ham, or any leftover cooked meat, and heat through before adding gravy.

Cooking times and common cuts

The following is a list of the cooking times and cutting directions for vegetables that are frequently stir-fried. There will be slight variations depending on the way the vegetable is cut, the amount of heat, the type of pan, the freshness of the vegetable, and the vegetable's natural texture.

Don't let these variables discourage you. The temptation to turn down the heat, clap on a lid, and turn your attention to last-minute chores, leaving the vegetables to take care of themselves, is almost irresistible to most non-Orientals. But the feeling for, and the taste for vegetables cooked Oriental-style comes surprisingly quickly. After a few tries, you'll get the feel of it on your own stove with your own pan. After a little bit of practice, you'll be able to stir-fry vegetables and experiment with combinations and seasonings with whatever you have on hand.

✔ Asparagus. Roll-cut or cut in ¼-inch-diagonal slices. Stir-fry 1 minute. Add 2 tablespoons water. Cover for 1 or 2 minutes.

✔ Arrowhead. Peel; slice or cut in half and mash lightly with broad side of cleaver. Stir-fry 1 minute. Add 2 tablespoons water. Cover for 3 to 4 minutes.

✔ Bamboo shoots, canned. Dice, slice, or cut in matchstick strips. Stir-fry 2 to 3 minutes.

✔ Bean sprouts (mung). Leave whole. Stir-fry 1 minute. Season with a few drops sesame oil and vinegar.

✔ Bean sprouts (soy). Leave whole, stir-fry 1½ to 2 minutes.

Slicing is quick work with Japanese vegetable slicer. Blade adjusts to regulate thickness of each slice.

Use interchangeable comb-like blade for shredding. Cut daikon, carrots, in fine, medium, or coarse shreds.

Cut vegetables with Japanese cutters or aspic cutters when you want to add a decorative garnish to any dish.

✔Bitter melon. Cut in half, scoop out seeds, and cut in ¼-inch-thick slices. Parboil 3 minutes to reduce bitter flavor. Stir-fry 1 minute with 1 clove minced garlic and 1 teaspoon minced fermented black beans. Add 2 tablespoons water. Cover for 3 to 4 minutes.

✔Bok choy. Cut diagonally in 1-inch slices. Stir-fry 1 minute. Add 2 tablespoons water. Cover for 1½ to 2 minutes. For tender inner hearts of *bok choy,* cook 1 minute after covering.

✔Broccoli. Cut into flowerets. Split heavy stems; cut 1 inch long. Stir-fry 1 minute. Add 2 tablespoons water. Cover for 3 to 4 minutes.

✔Broccoli (Chinese). Cut in 2-inch-long pieces. Stir-fry 1 minute. Add 2 tablespoons water. Cover for 2 minutes. Add 2 tablespoons oyster sauce to gravy.

✔Beans, Chinese long. Cut in 1½-inch lengths. Stir-fry 1 minute. Add 2 tablespoons water. Cover 2 to 3 minutes. One chopped chili pepper and 2 teaspoons brown bean sauce are a good flavor addition.

✔Beans, green. Cut in 1-inch lengths. Stir-fry 1 minute. Add 2 tablespoons water. Cover for 3 to 4 minutes.

✔Cabbage, Chinese. Split lower stalks lengthwise; cut in 1-inch slices. Cut leaves in 1-inch slices. Stir-fry 1 minute. Add 2 tablespoons water. Cover for 2 minutes.

✔Cabbage (regular). Cut in ½-inch slices. Stir-fry 1 minute. Add 1 tablespoon water. Cover for 2 minutes.

✔Cabbage, mustard. Cut in 1-inch slices. Stir-fry 1 minute. Add 1 tablespoon water. Cover for 2 minutes. With broadleaf mustard cabbage, use thick stems; cut crosswise in ¼-inch-thick slices. Stir-fry 1 minute. Add 1 tablespoon water. Toss for 1 to 2 minutes.

✔Carrots. Cut in ⅛-inch-thick diagonal slices or matchstick strips. Stir-fry 1 minute. Add 2 tablespoons water. Cover for 3 to 4 minutes.

✔Cauliflower. Cut into flowerets. If large, split in half lengthwise. Stir-fry 1 minute. Add 2 tablespoons water. Cover 3 to 4 minutes.

✔Celery. Diced, in chunks, or diagonal slices. Stir-fry 2 minutes.

✔Chayote. Cut in half lengthwise, peel, and thinly slice. Stir-fry 1 minute. Add 2 tablespoons water. Cover for 3 to 4 minutes.

✔Chinese okra. Peel off ridges; leave some of green peel between the ridges. Roll-cut. Stir-fry 1 minute. Add 1 tablespoon water. Toss for 1 to 2 minutes.

✔Eggplant, Oriental. Do not peel. Roll-cut or cut in cubes. Stir-fry 1 minute. Add 2 to 3 tablespoons water. Cover for 4 to 5 minutes.

✔Kohlrabi. Slice, dice, or cut in thin wedges. Stir-fry 1 minute. Add 2 tablespoons water. Cover 3 minutes.

✔Lettuce, iceberg. Tear off as for salad. Stir-fry 1 minute.

✔Lotus root. Peel and thinly slice. Stir-fry 1 minute. Add 2 tablespoons water. Cover for 2 to 3 minutes.

✔Mushrooms, dried. Presoak 30 minutes, squeeze dry, remove stems, slice. Stir-fry 1 minute. Add 1 tablespoon water and 1 teaspoon soy sauce. Cover for 2 minutes.

✔Mushrooms, fresh. Slice. Stir-fry 1 minute. Add 1 tablespoon water and 1 teaspoon soy sauce. Cover 1 minute. Remove cover, toss 1 minute.

✔Onions. Slice or cut in wedges. Stir-fry 1 to 2 minutes.

✔Peas, edible pod. Leave whole. Stir-fry 1 minute. Add 1 tablespoon water. Toss for 1 to 2 minutes.

✔Peas, fresh or frozen. Shell fresh peas; thaw frozen peas. Stir-fry 1 minute. Add 1 tablespoon water. Toss 1 minute.

✔Peppers, red and green. Cut in chunks or strips. Stir-fry 1 minute. Add 2 teaspoons water. Toss 1 minute.

✔Spinach. Wash; remove tough stem ends. Cut leaves in 2-inch strips. Stir-fry 1 minute. Cover for 1 minute.

✔Squash, baseball bat. Quarter lengthwise and cut in ¼-inch-thick slices. Stir-fry 1 minute. Add 2 tablespoons water. Cover 3 minutes.

✔Swiss chard. Cut in 1-inch strips. Stir-fry 1 minute. Add 1 tablespoon water. Cover for 2 minutes.

✔Tomatoes. Cut in wedges. Stir-fry 1 to 1½ minutes.

✔Turnips. Slice or dice. Stir-fry 1 minute. Add 2 tablespoons water. Cover for 2 to 3 minutes.

✔Water chestnuts, canned. Slice. Stir-fry 1 minute.

✔Water chestnuts, fresh. Peel and slice. Stir-fry 1 minute. Add 1 tablespoon water. Cover 2 minutes.

✔Watercress. Wash, trim tough stems. Stir-fry 1 to 1½ minutes.

✔Winter melon. Peel; cut in cubes or slices. Stir-fry 1 minute. Add 2 tablespoons water. Cover for 3 minutes.

✔Zucchini or summer squash. Roll-cut. Stir-fry 1 minute. Add 2 tablespoons water. Cover for 2 minutes.

Other ways with vegetables

Personally, I'm so smitten with stir-fried vegetables that I don't often remember that there are all kinds of other ways to go. Whenever I use these recipes, I wonder why I don't use them more often.

Baked Sato Imo — Japanese Taro

Japanese *taros* are rather small, like new potatoes. They weigh in at about five to the pound. We like them baked. They taste like a creamy stuffed potato without all the work involved. Wash *taro*, peel, and rinse. (If you don't plan to cook it immediately cover with water.) Bake in a hot oven (400°) until *taro* feels soft when squeezed, about 35 minutes.

Baked Chinese Taro

This is much larger than the Japanese *taro*, is coarser in texture, and is also delicious baked.

Cut *taro* lengthwise in wedges. Bake in a hot oven (400°) until soft, about 1 hour. Serve with butter, salt, and pepper.

Fish-Flavored Eggplant

Every year we look forward to the first Oriental eggplant in our garden. This spicy dish contains no fish—but the garlic and ginger are frequently used to season Chinese fish.

  2 tablespoons salad oil
  1½ tablespoons *each* minced garlic
    and ginger root
  ¼ cup minced pork
  1 large green onion and top, finely
    chopped
  2 Oriental eggplants, cut in bite-size
    pieces, roll-cut (3 cups eggplant)
  ½ cup chicken stock
  2 tablespoons soy sauce
  1 teaspoon sugar
  1 teaspoon sesame oil
  1 teaspoon cornstarch mixed with 1
    tablespoon water

1. Heat wok; add oil and heat. Add garlic and ginger; stir-fry 30 seconds. Remove from wok and reserve.

2. Add pork and stir-fry over high heat for 3 minutes. Return garlic and ginger to pan along with green onion and eggplant. Stir-fry for 2 minutes.

3. Add chicken stock, soy sauce, sugar, and sesame oil. Cover and simmer for 5 to 6 minutes. Stir cornstarch mixture to recombine, add to pan, and stir until thickened, about 30 seconds. Serves 4.

Barbecued Eggplant

When I am barbecuing *teriyaki* steak or chicken, I like to cook the whole unpeeled Oriental eggplant alongside. The flavor is good and it has very few calories. Use low coals and cook until soft, about 10 minutes on each side. Serve with grated *daikon* or grated ginger root and soy sauce.

Hasame Yaki — Eggplant with Chicken

  1 whole chicken breast, boned and
    skinned
  6 Oriental eggplants
    Salad oil
  ¼ cup soy sauce
  2 tablespoons sherry
  1 tablespoon sugar
  1 small clove garlic, minced
  ½ teaspoon grated ginger root
  1 teaspoon cornstarch mixed with 1
    tablespoon water

1. Cut each half of chicken breast lengthwise in thirds to get 6 strips. Cut eggplant in half lengthwise to within 2 inches of the stem end. Fit a strip of chicken inside each eggplant. Rub oil over eggplant.

2. Combine soy sauce, sherry, sugar, garlic, and ginger in a saucepan. Simmer for 3 minutes. Stir cornstarch and water to recombine, add to pan, and stir—cook until thickened.

3. Broil eggplant 5 to 7 inches from the heat, 6 minutes on each side.

Or bake in a moderately hot oven (375°) until tender, about 25 minutes. Brush sauce over eggplant and broil for a few seconds to glaze. Serves 6.

Stuffed Cabbage

  6 large Chinese cabbage leaves
  ¼ pound ground pork
  ⅓ pound ground chicken
  1 teaspoon cornstarch
  ½ teaspoon salt
  ¼ teaspoon monosodium glutamate
  2 dried mushrooms, presoaked
    and minced
  24 inches of *kampyo* (dried gourd
    strips), presoaked 10 minutes

Cooking Stock:

  2 cups chicken stock mixed with
    1 teaspoon *each* soy sauce and
    sherry, ½ teaspoon *each* salt and
    sugar, and a dash of monosodium
    glutamate
  4 dried mushrooms, presoaked
    30 minutes
  4 broccoli flowerets, parboiled
    4 minutes and drained

1. Cook leaves in a small amount of water for 3 minutes; drain.

2. Combine pork, chicken, cornstarch, salt, monosodium glutamate, and minced mushrooms.

3. Lay cabbage leaves on a *sudare* so they cover the entire mat. The leaves should run parallel to the ribs of the mat forming a 9x9-inch layer. Shape meat to form a roll 9 inches long and place across middle of cabbage. Roll mat like a jelly roll so the cabbage encases the filling. Tie roll in 8 places tightly with strips of *kampyo*. Place in a large frying pan.

4. Pour cooking stock over roll. Cover and simmer for 30 minutes. Remove roll from stock and cool slightly. Cook mushrooms in stock for 15 minutes.

5. To serve, cut cabbage roll crosswise in 8 pieces. Arrange 2 slices in each bowl and garnish each serving with a mushroom and a piece of broccoli. Serves 4.

Many countries serve stuffed cabbage; the Japanese do it with elegance.

Serve one hasame yaki *as first course, two for an entreé. Ginger adds zest.*

If you want to add variety to an easy oven meal, try baked Chinese taro.

Beef and pork dishes

**You won't find a roast waiting to be carved on an Oriental dinner table.
Meat is cut and cooked in bite-size pieces to accommodate chopsticks.
Traditionally, meat is not so much the basis for a meal as it is a complement.**

While putting this chapter together, I was faced with a recurring question: Is this a meat recipe, or is this a vegetable recipe?

The same kind of question comes up at meal-planning time. If I cook broccoli beef, do I serve it as a meat or as a vegetable? And what should I serve with it—a meat? Or a vegetable?

For cooks who are accustomed to planning a menu around a piece of meat and filling in the cracks with a vegetable, a starch, and a salad, it's puzzling to know just how to fit an Oriental dish into a Western meal. How does the cook (and mama) provide the protein Americans expect?

Meat with vegetables

My family solved it for me. When I first started Chinese cooking, I stuck to one dish at a time, plus rice, so we simply ate less meat at that particular meal. No one seemed to mind. The flavor of vegetables cooked in an Oriental way is so satisfying that we found we did not need to have every meal high in red meat protein.

Recently I stir-fried a big batch of beef with no vegetables at all, thinking I was preparing a special treat. We were surprised how our tastes had changed. It seemed almost too rich—like eating only the frosting on a cake.

In some of the stir-fried recipes the amount of meat called for is on the low side. You *can* do what the Chinese do—serve several different main dishes, each one accented with a bit of meat, fish, or poultry—but I don't recommend it, at least at first.

◁

Chinese chives add color and flavor to pork and liver. (Recipe page 63.)

That makes it such a full-scale production that you won't do it often, and won't get around to trying some really delicious dishes. Or you can do what our family did: relax and enjoy each dish one by one.

Oriental shopping

Oriental cooking takes some adjustment in shopping and storage habits, too. A recipe may call for only four or eight ounces of meat. American stores are scaled to big buying and prepackaged meat.

Once in a while I get loose in an Oriental market where I can buy a dab of this and a snip of that, but usually I buy in slabs and chunks, bring it home, cut it up, package it in recipe-scaled amounts, and freeze it. I particularly like to do this with flank steak and a pork butt, cutting a flank in half lengthwise for two meals and cutting the pork in half-pound pieces for several.

You will note that in many recipes I have specified only "boneless pork." The Chinese like pork butt. One Oriental friend always uses a fatty cut so it won't taste dry and scratchy; another friend always trims the meat well; another chooses a lean cut, such as pork loin. I usually use whatever's on hand, and I try to keep pork butt on hand.

Though these recipes are low on meat by American standards, they might be high on meat by Oriental ones. A Chinese friend who grew up in Hawaii recalls that her mother would cut a flank steak in three parts, for three dinners, for five people. I literally can't cut my meat that thin (by habit); *half* a flank steak for five people is as far as I can go.

But do not consider these meat amounts law. Adjust upward or downward to suit your own tastes, budget, pantry. Remember as you extemporize on these recipes or create favorites of your own that in traditional Oriental cooking the meat is not so much the basis as it is a *complement*—then establish some traditions of your own.

When estimating the number of

Oyster sauce goes into Broccoli Beef just before serving. (Recipe page 62.)

1. Pork and Liver with Gow Choy begins with slicing the meat and vegetables.

2. Stir-fry pork, add onion, and cook 2 minutes. Remove mixture from the wok.

3. Stir-fry liver quickly so it is just charred on the outside, juicy inside.

servings for each recipe, I have treated the recipe as a main dish to be served with rice. Naturally when you prepare several main dishes for an Oriental meal, you can count on more servings per dish.

Stir-frying

Almost all stir-fried dishes invite endless improvization. Once you have mastered the basic techniques you can take off on your own. The components are simple: a meat, a marinade, a vegetable (or several), and a gravy. In stir-frying a good proportion to use is one part meat to two parts vegetables.

A word of caution: Be sure not to overcrowd the pan. The meat should brown quickly, not stew juicily. If I am using more than a cup of meat, I cook it in two batches, making sure that the oil is very hot when I toss in the meat.

And a word of challenge. Start cooking as the Orientals do—using as few dishes as possible. My friend Jeanette seasons the meat on the cutting board, for one thing.

Vegetables for stir-fried beef

Some of these are traditional combinations. Some are from friends. Some were born of expedience.

Broccoli Beef

Follow the basic recipe, using 4 cups broccoli, regular or Chinese. Separate stalks and flowers. Cut flowers into bite-size pieces. Strip outer fibers from stalks; cut stalks diagonally in pieces ¼ inch thick. If stalks are thick, split in half lengthwise before cutting. Stir in 2 tablespoons oyster sauce after gravy thickens.

Asparagus Beef

Bend asparagus until stalks break; discard tough ends. Cut diagonally in pieces ¼ inch thick. Follow basic recipe.

Zucchini Beef

Roll-cut zucchini. Follow basic recipe. As a variation, add one onion.

Ginger Beef

Follow basic recipe, but omit minced ginger from marinade, and eliminate vegetables. Instead, use ¼-cup thinly sliced ginger root, stir-frying it with the meat. Toss ¼-cup green onions and tops, cut in 1-inch lengths, into pan 30 seconds before adding gravy ingredients.

Oyster Sauce Beef

Follow basic recipe, using ½ pound fresh mushrooms (whole if small, sliced if large). Omit water. Stir in ¼ cup Chinese chives, cut in ½-inch lengths, just before adding gravy. Stir in 2 tablespoons oyster sauce after gravy thickens.

Other Vegetables. Consider cauliflower, *bok choy,* Chinese cabbage, edible podded peas, yard-long beans, string beans, bitter melon, fuzzy melon, celery—alone or in combination. Cut the vegetables in approximately the same size so they will all finish cooking at the same time. If you prefer less gravy, cut the amount in half.

Basic Stir-fried Beef

You can use flank steak, boneless chuck roast, or top round; flank steak is the most tender. On occasion I use beef heart, thinly sliced.

1 pound boneless beef

Marinade:
1 tablespoon soy sauce
1 tablespoon cornstarch
½ teaspoon salt
2 teaspoons sherry or rice wine
1 clove garlic, minced
2 thin slices ginger root, minced or grated
   Salad oil for frying
4 cups cut vegetables (see suggestions right; also see page 56 for ways to cut vegetables)
2 tablespoons water (optional; depends upon water content of vegetable)

Gravy:
1 tablespoon *each* cornstarch and soy sauce mixed with ½ cup water

1. Cut meat in strips 2 inches wide. Holding blade at 45° angle, slice each strip across the grain in ¼-inch-thick pieces. Season (on the board) with soy sauce, cornstarch, salt, sherry, garlic, and ginger. Let stand 15 minutes.

2. Heat a wok or frying pan. Pour in 2 tablespoons oil, swirl it about in the pan, and heat. Add beef; stir-fry over high heat until browned outside, pink inside, about 2 minutes. (Cook in two batches if pan does not stay hot enough.) Remove from pan.

3. Heat 2 tablespoons oil in same pan. Add vegetables and stir-fry about 2 minutes. Sprinkle with salt. If you are using vegetables that are very firm, add 2 tablespoons water and cover if necessary. Cook vegetables only until crisp-tender. Return meat to pan. Stir gravy to recombine, pour into pan, and cook until thickened, about 30 seconds. Serves 5 to 6 as a main course with rice.

4. *Add gow choy (Chinese chives) to wok and give a quick stir with the liver.*

5. *Stir in soy sauce. Return pork and onion to wok and stir-fry 30 seconds.*

6. *It is ready for serving in 6 minutes. Short cooking keeps the color bright.*

Pork and Liver with Gow Choy

If you try no other recipe in this book, and if you have trouble selling liver at your house, I hope you'll try this recipe.

My sons like liver no better than the next fellow, but even so, this is one of our favorite meals. I failed three times before I learned to cook it; I figured that a liver dish that everyone likes was worth being stubborn about. It takes lots of oil so the liver won't stick, and if you cut the liver too thin it will dry out. *Gow choy* is available only in Chinese markets but it's easy to grow (see vegetable gardening chapter)—a cut-and-come-again chive.

    1 teaspoon cornstarch
    1 tablespoon soy sauce
    ¼ teaspoon *each* white pepper and
        sugar
    ⅔ pound boneless pork, cut in slices
        1 inch wide, 2 inches long, and
        ⅛-inch thick
        Salad oil for frying
    ¼ teaspoon salt
    1 small onion, cut in half lengthwise,
        then in crosswise slices ¼ inch thick
    ⅔ pound beef liver, cut in slices 1 inch
        wide, 2 inches long, and ¼ inch thick
    1 bunch *gow choy* (Chinese chives),
        cut in 2-inch lengths (about ⅔ cup)
    1 tablespoon soy sauce

1. Sprinkle cornstarch, soy sauce, pepper, and sugar over pork.

2. Heat 2 tablespoons oil in a wok or large frying pan. Sprinkle with salt, add pork, and stir-fry over high heat for 2 minutes. Add onion; continue cooking until pork loses its reddish color, about 2 minutes. Remove.

3. Heat 4 tablespoons oil in the same pan. Add liver and stir-fry over high heat for 1½ minutes; it should be almost charred on the outside, tender and juicy inside. Stir in *gow choy* and soy sauce. Return pork and onion to pan. Reheat, stirring for 30 seconds. Serves 4 to 6.

Sweet and Sour Pineapple Spareribs

    2 pounds spareribs
    1 tablespoon *each* soy sauce and sherry
    1 teaspoon sugar
    ½ teaspoon salt
    2 teaspoons cornstarch
    1 clove garlic, minced
    1 slice ginger root, minced
        Salad oil for frying
    1 onion, cut in wedges; layers separated
    1 small green pepper, cut in chunks
    1 flat can (8 oz.) sliced pineapple cut
        in wedges (save juice)

Gravy:
        Pineapple juice and enough water to
        make ¾ cup liquid
    3 tablespoons catsup
    2 tablespoons *each* sugar and vinegar
    ¼ teaspoon salt
    1 tablespoon cornstarch

1. Ask the meat man to cut ribs in 1-inch lengths. Trim fat and cut between the bones. Marinate in soy sauce, sherry, sugar, salt, cornstarch, garlic, and ginger for 1 hour.

2. Heat 2 tablespoons oil in a large frying pan. Brown ribs well, then reduce heat, cover, and cook for 30 minutes. Stir several times during cooking. Remove from pan and drain on paper toweling. Pour out pan drippings and rinse pan.

3. Heat 1 tablespoon oil in same pan: Add onion and green pepper and stir-fry over high heat for 2 minutes. Add drained pineapple and meat and stir-fry for 2 minutes. Pour in the combined gravy ingredients; cook, stirring, until thickened. Serves 6.

Sweet and Sour Pineapple Pork

Follow the above recipe, substituting boneless pork for spareribs. Cut meat in 1-inch squares, marinate, and cook for 40 minutes after browning.

Melting Spareribs with Black Bean Sauce

When the Chinese perfected this method of cooking spareribs, they couldn't have known about my constant kitchen interruptions, but I am grateful to them for such an interruptible dish. When I'm feeding people in shifts or if dinner is delayed, or if I'm trying to assemble an entire Oriental meal, I just turn off the heat and re-steam the ribs as needed. The longer they steam, the more tender the meat.

    2 pounds spareribs, cut in 1-inch
        lengths
    2 tablespoons fermented black beans
    1 large garlic clove, peeled
    ¼-inch slice ginger root
    1½ tablespoons soy sauce
    1½ tablespoons cornstarch
    ¼ teaspoon salt

1. Trim excess fat from spareribs and cut between the bones.

2. Place black beans in a sieve and rinse with water. Mince together with garlic and ginger. Place with soy sauce, cornstarch, and salt in a casserole or shallow bowl large enough to hold spareribs and mix.

3. Put spareribs in bowl and turn several times to coat with bean mixture. Steam on a rack in a covered pan for 1 hour to 1 hour and 15 minutes, stirring every 15 minutes. Serves 4 to 6.

Oriental Barbecued Pork

This is a cross-cultural variation of *char siu* with Chinese and Japanese flavors.

    4 pounds boneless pork butt or
        4 pounds spareribs
    ½ cup soy sauce
    ¼ cup brown sugar
    ½ teaspoon salt
    ¼ teaspoon monosodium glutamate
    1 large clove garlic, minced
    2 tablespoons catsup

1. Cut pork in 1-inch-thick slices. Or cut spareribs between the bones in 3-inch sections.

2. Mix soy sauce, brown sugar, salt, monosodium glutamate, garlic, and catsup. Pour over meat and marinate for 4 hours.

3. Remove meat from marinade and arrange on a broiling rack set in a roasting pan. Roast in a moderate oven (350°) for 1 hour. Turn meat several times during cooking and brush with marinade. Thinly slice meat or cut sparerib sections into individual ribs. If ribs are large, chop each in half crosswise. Serves 8.

Pork Roast with Miso

This recipe, from a Japanese cook who grew up in Hawaii, is reminiscent of Island-style pork cooked in a pit. The meat is so tender it almost falls apart in shreds.

½ cup *miso* (white soybean paste)
⅓ cup sugar
½ cup soy sauce
2 cups water
2 cloves garlic, mashed
2 thin slices ginger root, mashed
3 pounds boneless pork roast

1. In a saucepan blend the *miso*, sugar, soy sauce, and water until smooth. Add the garlic, ginger, and meat.

2. Cover pan, bring to a boil, then simmer for 3 hours or until meat is tender. Turn meat in sauce several times during cooking. Serves 6.

Char Siu — Chinese Barbecued Pork

The very best *char siu* is the kind you buy—at least that is what many of my Chinese friends say. There is even disagreement over whether the *very best* is made in San Francisco or Honolulu. It is true that without a special oven it is difficult to produce the characteristic red coloring. But it has no secret flavor that can't easily be duplicated at home.

I make it in a rather large quantity because the meat is good for so many things. Slice it and serve warm as it comes from the oven, use it as a garnish for soup, noodles, or fried rice, or serve it cold with drinks.

¼ cup soy sauce
2 teaspoons five-spice powder
3 tablespoons sherry
2 teaspoons salt
½ cup sugar
1½ tablespoons red bean curd
½ teaspoon red food coloring
4 pounds boneless pork butt, cut in 1-inch-thick slices

1. Combine soy sauce, five-spice powder, sherry, salt, sugar, bean curd, and food coloring. Marinate meat for at least 6 hours.

2. Remove meat from marinade, place on a rack set inside a pan, and roast in a moderate oven (350°) for 1 hour. Turn several times during cooking and brush with marinade. Cut in thin slices and serve hot or cold.

The variations are many with the recipe for minced pork. Here it steams in bitter melon slices (recipe below).

Steamed Minced Pork

1 pound boneless pork, ground or finely minced
4 water chestnuts, finely chopped
1 tablespoon soy sauce
2 teaspoons cornstarch
½ teaspoon *each* salt and sugar
Dash of pepper
1 teaspoon salad oil (add only if you use a very lean cut of pork)

Mix all ingredients thoroughly. Form into a thin pancake in a shallow bowl or on a plate with a rim. Place in a steamer, and steam for 45 minutes. Serves 4.

Variations for Steamed Minced Pork

The basic recipe above can be varied by adding one of the seasonings listed below. Combine with uncooked pork and proceed as in basic recipe. You can also use all of the pork mixtures as stuffings (see below).

✓Dried mushrooms. Presoak 4 large mushrooms 30 minutes, squeeze out water, and finely chop.

✓Ham. Finely chop ¼ pound.

✓Salted cabbage (*chung choy*). Finely chop 1x2-inch piece.

✓Chinese sausage (*lop cheong*). Finely chop 2 sausages.

Stuffed Bitter Melon

Use one-half recipe for Steamed Minced Pork or a variation. Cut 2 bitter melons in rounds 1 inch thick; remove seeds. Stuff with meat mixture. Dip filled slices on each side in cornstarch; brown lightly in 1 tablespoon oil. Arrange on a plate rubbed with a little sesame oil. Steam 40 minutes.

Stuffed Green Peppers

Cut 2 green peppers in quarters and rub lightly with salad oil. Stuff with one-half recipe Steamed Minced Pork or one of the variations. Arrange on a plate; steam 40 minutes.

Stuffed Bean Cake

Mix one-half recipe Steamed Minced Pork with finely chopped Chinese sausage. Cut 16 small squares fried bean cake (*dow foo pok*) in half crosswise. Stuff meat mixture inside bean cakes. Arrange filled cakes on two plates. Drizzle 1 tablespoon salad oil over the tops. Place in a steamer and steam for 40 minutes. If you do not have a double steaming basket, steam one batch, then the other. You can reheat the first batch in just a few minutes.

Pork and Oysters in Lettuce Packets

For some reason I have never served this with an Oriental meal though it would be good. It's my answer to the chips-and-dips blahs. It cooks quickly so you can easily leave your guests for a few minutes. (Assemble everything early in the day and refrigerate it.) I spoon the hot filling into small teacups, set them on plates with a few lettuce leaves, and provide small spoons so each person can assemble his own. If I am serving guests who have very conservative tastes, I leave out the dried oysters and substitute cooked, small baby shrimp.

>   2 tablespoons salad oil
> ¼ teaspoon salt
> ½ pound boneless pork, diced, and mixed with 1 teaspoon *each* cornstarch and soy sauce
> ¼ cup chopped celery
> ½ cup chopped onion
>   3 water chestnuts, diced
> ¼ cup diced bamboo shoots
>   4 dried mushrooms, presoaked and diced (save soaking liquid)
>   4 dried oysters (optional), soaked in water for 24 hours, washed, and diced
> 15 edible podded peas, ends and strings removed, and coarsely chopped, *or*
> ½ cup defrosted frozen peas
>   2 tablespoons oyster sauce
>   1 tablespoon cornstarch mixed with 1 tablespoon water
>   Iceberg lettuce leaves, washed and chilled

1. Heat oil in a wok or frying pan. Sprinkle with salt, add pork, and stir-fry over high heat for 2 minutes. Reduce heat and cook for 2 minutes.

2. Increase heat and add celery, onion, water chestnuts, bamboo shoots, mushrooms, and oysters. Stir-fry 1 minute. Add 2 tablespoons of the mushroom soaking liquid if mixture seems dry. Add peas and cook for 1 minute.

3. Add oyster sauce. Stir cornstarch water mixture, pour into pan, and cook until thickened. To eat, wrap each bite inside a lettuce leaf. Serves 6.

Mu Shu Pork— Pork with Lily Buds and Egg

This pork mixture is usually folded inside a Mandarin pancake. (Or look in the frozen food section of your market for *lumpia* or egg roll wrappers; you can use them instead. Do not try to use the noodle squares for spring rolls.) The doilies are about 8 inches across and very very thin. To reheat the thawed wrappers, follow the directions for steaming Mandarin pancakes (right). Since the wrappers dry out quickly in reheating I sometimes serve them at room tem-

perature. The filling is sizzling hot and the contrast is fine.

> ½ cup dried lily buds
>   5 dried cloud ear mushrooms
>   Salad oil for frying
>   3 eggs, beaten with ¼ teaspoon salt
> ½ pound boneless pork, cut in matchstick strips and coated with 1 teaspoon cornstarch, and 1 tablespoon *each* soy sauce and sherry
> ¼ teaspoon salt
>   1 teaspoon minced ginger root
> ½ pound bean sprouts, washed and drained
>   Mandarin pancakes or *lumpia* wrappers
>   *Hoisin* sauce or plum sauce
>   3 green onions, cut in 1½-inch lengths and shredded

1. Soak lily buds in warm water for 30 minutes; drain, break off tough stem ends, and cut each bud in half. Soak cloud ears in warm water for 30 minutes; snap off hard stems, wash, and cut in ¼-inch-thick strips.

2. Heat 1 tablespoon oil in a wok or frying pan. Add eggs and scramble over medium low heat until soft curds form. Transfer to a bowl and break up with a fork. Rinse wok.

3. Heat 2 tablespoons oil. Add pork and stir-fry for 4 minutes. Add lily buds and cloud ears and stir-fry 1 minute. Reduce heat and cook for 2 minutes. Remove from pan.

4. Heat 2 tablespoons oil and sprinkle with the ¼ teaspoon salt. Add ginger and stir around pan once. Immediately add bean sprouts and stir-fry 2 minutes. Return pork mixture and eggs and stir-fry only to reheat.

Each person puts a little *hoisin* or plum sauce on a pancake, spoons on some of the pork filling, adds green onions if desired, and rolls and folds the wrapper around the filling. Makes enough to fill 12 wrappers.

Mandarin Pancakes

>   2 cups sifted all-purpose flour
> ¾ cup boiling water
>   2 tablespoons sesame oil or salad oil

1. Place flour in a bowl, make a well in the center, and pour in boiling water. Mix with a fork to form a soft dough. Turn onto a lightly floured board and knead lightly for 10 minutes or until smooth. Cover and let rest for 15 minutes.

2. Divide dough into 12 equal pieces. Cover with plastic film.

3. To make each pancake, cut a piece of the dough in half. Roll both halves on a lightly floured board to make two circles 3 inches in diameter. Brush oil lightly on top of one circle, cover with the other circle, and press the two together, making a pair (which will be separated after cooking).

4. Roll out the double round to form a circle 7 or 8 inches in diameter, rotating the round as you roll so the circle keeps its shape. (Don't worry if you don't get perfect circles.) Repeat procedure to make each pancake. Keep uncooked pancakes covered.

5. Heat a large frying pan over medium heat and cook pancakes, a pair at a time, in the ungreased pan. Turn them every 15 seconds as little bubbles appear on the surface. The pancake should be the color of parchment, only slightly speckled; it should feel dry. It becomes brittle if overcooked. As you finish each pancake, carefully separate the layers and stack them on a plate. Keep covered as you cook remaining cakes. Serve at once or wrap in foil and refrigerate or freeze for later use.

6. To reheat, place in a steamer and steam for 5 minutes. Fold pancakes in triangles and arrange in serving basket. Since they dry out quickly, do not oversteam. Makes 24.

Chinese sausage is one of the many things you can buy for a quick meal at Oriental markets. Steam sausage for 15 minutes, slice, serve with rice. Dip sausage in mustard, soy sauce.

Buta Dofu — Pork with Tofu

A combination of pork and *tofu* makes this dish doubly high in protein. Serve it with *sunomono* (a Japanese "salad" see page 39) and rice.

1 pound square *tofu* (soybean cake)
2 teaspoons salad oil
½ pound boneless pork, cut in strips
   ¼ inch thick, ½ inch wide, and
   1½ inches long
1 large onion, cut in half lengthwise
   and sliced crosswise in ¼-inch-
   thick slices
¾ cup water
2 tablespoons *shiro miso* (white soybean paste)
2 teaspoons *fu yu* (fermented
   bean cake)
3 tablespoons soy sauce
5 green onions and tops, cut in
   1½-inch lengths
20 edible podded peas, ends and side
   strings removed
2 teaspoons cornstarch mixed with
   1 tablespoon water

1. Cut *tofu* in pieces ½ x ½ x 1½ inches; drain in colander.

2. Heat oil in a large frying pan; add pork, and stir and cook over medium heat for 5 minutes. Add onion slices and cook 2 minutes.

3. Combine water, *miso,* fermented bean cake, and soy sauce; blend until smooth, then pour over meat. Push meat to side of pan and add *tofu;* spoon meat over *tofu* and combine gently. Simmer 5 minutes. Add green onions and peas, stir gently, and cook 2 minutes.

4. Stir cornstarch-water mixture to recombine it, pour into pan, and cook until sauce thickens. Serves 4 to 6.

Kombu Maki with Pork

In Japanese grocery stores you can buy small rolls of preseasoned *kombu* that require a little cooking and can be served as appetizers. Many are seasoned with tiny dried fish. Or you can make this variation with a pork filling.

50 inches of *kombu* (dried kelp) 3 to
   4 inches wide
   Kampyo (dried gourd strips)
½ pound boneless pork
3 cups water
⅓ cup soy sauce
1 teaspoon salt
3 tablespoons sugar
½ teaspoon monosodium glutamate

1. Soak *kombu* in water for 15 minutes. Cut in 2½-inch-wide strips. If *kombu* is wider than 4 inches, cut in half to make 2 pieces. Soak *kampyo* in water for 15 minutes.

2. Cut pork in about 20 strips each 2½ inches long. Place a piece of pork on one edge of *kombu,* roll up to make a log, and tie with a piece of *kampyo.* Continue until you have used all the *kombu* and meat.

3. Place rolls in a saucepan with water; cover and simmer for 2½ hours. Add soy sauce, salt, sugar, and monosodium glutamate, and continue cooking for 30 minutes. Serve warm or cooled. Makes 20.

Kare — Beef Curry

It may surprise you—as it did me—that curry has been around a long time in Japan. One of my friends who grew up there said that when he was a teenager and frequented curry shops, he thought the Japanese had invented it. They did modify it, for this is very unlike Indian curry. The amount of meat is rather small, the amount of sauce large. Sometimes I add more vegetables—such as cubes of eggplant and green pepper—or sometimes I increase the amount of meat.

2 tablespoons salad oil
½ pound beef stew, cut in ¾-inch
   cubes
1 onion, cut in thin wedges, with
   layers separated
1 tablespoon curry powder
3½ cups water
1¼ teaspoons salt
1 teaspoon sugar
¼ teaspoon monosodium glutamate
1 tablespoon soy sauce
1 large carrot, peeled and cut in
   ½-inch-thick slices
2 medium potatoes, peeled and cut in
   bite-size pieces
3 tablespoons cornstarch mixed with
   ¼ cup water
   Red pickled ginger (*benishoga*)
   Rakkyo (pickled scallions)

1. Heat oil in a large saucepan, add meat, and brown on all sides. Add onion and cook until lightly browned. Sprinkle in curry powder, stir, and cook for 30 seconds.

2. Add water, salt, sugar, monosodium glutamate, and soy sauce; cover and simmer for 30 minutes.

3. Add carrot and potatoes (or any other vegetables), and continue cooking for 20 minutes or until vegetables are tender.

4. Stir cornstarch mixture to recombine it, pour into curry, and stirring, cook until thickened. Serve over hot cooked rice with ginger and *rakkyo* or other condiments. Serves 4 to 6.

Tonkatsu — Japanese Pork Cutlet

1 pound boneless pork, butt or loin
   Salt and pepper
   Flour
2 eggs, beaten with 2 tablespoons milk
   Panko (Japanese dried bread crumbs)
   or other coarsely ground dried
   bread crumbs
   Oil for deep-fat frying

1. Cut pork in slices ½ inch thick, then pound with a mallet or plate to ¼-inch thickness.

2. Sprinkle with salt and pepper. Coat with flour, dip in eggs, then cover with bread crumbs. Let stand 10 minutes for coating to dry slightly.

3. Cook in hot deep fat (360°) 5 to 7 minutes. (Cut into one cutlet to be sure meat has lost pink coloring.) Drain on paper towels.

4. Cut each cutlet into bite-size pieces, then lift the pieces to a serving plate and reassemble in the original cutlet shape. Garnish with finely grated carrot and *daikon* or finely shredded cabbage. Serve with bottled *Tonkatsu* sauce or prepare the following: ½ cup catsup mixed with 2 tablespoons soy sauce and 1 tablespoon Worcestershire. Serves 4.

Sukiyaki

Every time I prepare *sukiyaki* I am struck by the contrast between Chinese and Japanese cooking. There is none of the tumbling action of Chinese stir-frying. The Japanese put everything into the pan so it is aesthetically pleasing, and leave everything in its own special place. You can turn it over, but you shouldn't stir it around.

Kombu maki *with pork (recipe at left). Roll pork in piece of* kombu *(kelp).*

Tie rolls with kampyo *(dried gourd strips) before cooking and seasoning.*

Traditionally, *sukiyaki* is cooked at the table in a continuous process.

1½ to 2 pounds boneless beef (a tender cut, such as tenderloin, sirloin, or top round), sliced ⅛ inch thick
2 or 3 pieces beef suet to grease pan
2 onions, cut in half lengthwise, then cut in ¼-inch-thick slices
½ pound fresh mushrooms, sliced ¼-inch-thick
2 bunches green onions and tops, cut diagonally in 1½-inch lengths
1 pound spinach or *shungiku* (garland chrysanthemum), stems *removed* and leaves cut in 1½-inch lengths
1 cup sliced bamboo shoots
1 can (8 oz.) *shirataki* (yam threads)
1 pound square *tofu* (soybean cake), cut in 1-inch squares

Cooking Sauce:

½ cup soy sauce
3 tablespoons sugar
¼ cup *mirin* or sherry
¾ cup *dashi*, or beef broth, or water
½ teaspoon monosodium glutamate

1. Cut meat in 1x2-inch pieces. Arrange all ingredients except cooking sauce attractively on a large platter, keeping each item separate.

2. Combine soy sauce, sugar, *mirin, dashi,* and monosodium glutamate and stir until sugar dissolves. Pour into a small pitcher.

3. Heat the pan and rub it well with suet; remove suet. Place one-third of meat in pan in a single layer and cook just until it loses pinkness, then push into a corner of the pan. Add one-third of the vegetables, keeping individual vegetables in their own place. Pour one-third of cooking sauce into pan. Cook 3 to 5 minutes, turning vegetables over as necessary.

4. Before the pan becomes completely empty, add more ingredients and sauce. Keep successive servings cooking. Serves 4 to 6.

Niku Nabe— Meat in a Pan for One

This is the specialty of friends who own the Ginza restaurant in Monterey, California. It has also become a specialty of the chief cook in the Nix house—a family-style variation of *sukiyaki* for a household that often eats in shifts. It isn't as fancy as *sukiyaki,* which I consider a company meal, but it's a godsend for eating on the run.

4 to 6 ounces boneless beef (tenderloin, or top round) sliced ⅛ inch thick
2 slices onion, cut in half-rounds
1 large mushroom, sliced
2 slices bamboo shoots
3 squares *tofu*, 1 inch square
Handful coarsely chopped Chinese cabbage
Handful *shirataki* (yam threads)
⅔ cup *sukiyaki* cooking sauce (see recipe at left)
1 green onion, including top, cut diagonally in 1½-inch lengths

In an individual casserole or small pan arrange the meat, onion, mushroom, bamboo shoots, *tofu,* cabbage, and *shirataki* in separate piles. Repeat for each serving. Just before cooking, pour in sauce. Place on high heat, bring to a boil, turn each ingredient over in place; reduce heat to medium and cook 4 minutes. Add green onion and cook another 30 seconds. Serve with rice. Makes 1 serving.

Korean Beef

I have a special spot in my heart for this dish—not only because it's delicious but because it's the first Oriental dish I learned to cook by watching good Korean friends in action. They were generous with their secrets; they came to visit, eat, and *cook.* Because the meat is sliced so small that it would fall through a normal grill, Angie put the meat in a wire sandwich toaster, then barbecued it quickly.

Years later, we had it at the Bando Hotel in Seoul. They cooked it at the table on a gas-heated dome. We wrapped lettuce around either a spoonful of rice and a dab of hot paste or the spicy meat itself. Marvelous. I can't find that bean paste here; Chinese chili paste is a good substitute.

Nowadays, for guests, I barbecue it on a Genghis Khan dome, with fond memories of our sandwich turner days with the Chais.

1 pound boneless chuck roast, cut in 2-inch-wide strips, ⅛ inch thick
2 tablespoons salad oil
4 tablespoons soy sauce
2 cloves garlic, minced
⅛ teaspoon monosodium glutamate
1½ teaspoons vinegar
Dash pepper
1½ teaspoons crushed, toasted sesame seeds
¼ to ½ teaspoon cayenne pepper
1 green onion (including top), finely chopped

Marinate meat for 30 minutes in all remaining ingredients. Spread in a single layer on a Genghis Khan dome, or in a wire sandwich turner, and cook over low coals for 3 to 5 minutes.

Genghis Khan Barbecue

When I feel especially lazy and still want to entertain friends, I barbecue both meat and vegetables at the table on a Genghis Khan dome (see photograph on the cover). Sometimes I marinate the meat with the Korean Beef marinade or cook it plain and serve with a dipping sauce.

If you don't have a dome to use on a hibachi, cover the grill with hardware cloth to keep the pieces of food from falling through.

Dipping Sauce:

1 cup chicken stock
⅓ cup soy sauce
1 or 2 teaspoons grated ginger root

1 pound boneless beef (sirloin, top round, or chuck) sliced ⅛ inch thick; save a few pieces of beef fat
2 zucchini
1 bunch leeks
1 bunch spinach or *shungiku*
20 edible podded peas, tips and side strings removed
8 large mushrooms, cut lengthwise in ¼-inch thick slices
2 small green peppers, cut in quarters lengthwise

1. Mix dipping sauce and pour in 4 small bowls.

2. Cut sliced meat in 2x3-inch pieces. Cut zucchini lengthwise in ¼-inch-thick slices, then cut in 2-inch lengths. Wash and trim leeks, discarding the green leaves. Cut in 2-inch lengths; split each piece in half lengthwise. Remove spinach or *shungiku* stems; cut in 2-inch pieces.

3. To cook, heat the dome over low coals. Lay a strip of fat on top of the dome and heat until it sizzles. Set a few beef strips on the top part of the dome; place part of the vegetables around the bottom of the dome. Cook 3 or 4 minutes or until done. The vegetables should be fairly crisp.

4. Each person seasons the meat and vegetables with the dipping sauce. Keep successive servings cooking. Serves 4.

Teriyaki Sauce

This is a marinade for any meat or poultry; you can also use it to baste meat during barbecuing or broiling. Meat should marinate for at least one hour. (It's a tenderizer, too, so give less tender cuts a longer bath.)

1 cup soy sauce
¼ cup *sake, mirin,* or sherry
5 tablespoons sugar
2 cloves garlic, minced
1 teaspoon grated ginger root

Blend all ingredients, stirring until sugar dissolves. Do not keep leftover marinade—used—longer than a few days (because of the meat juices).

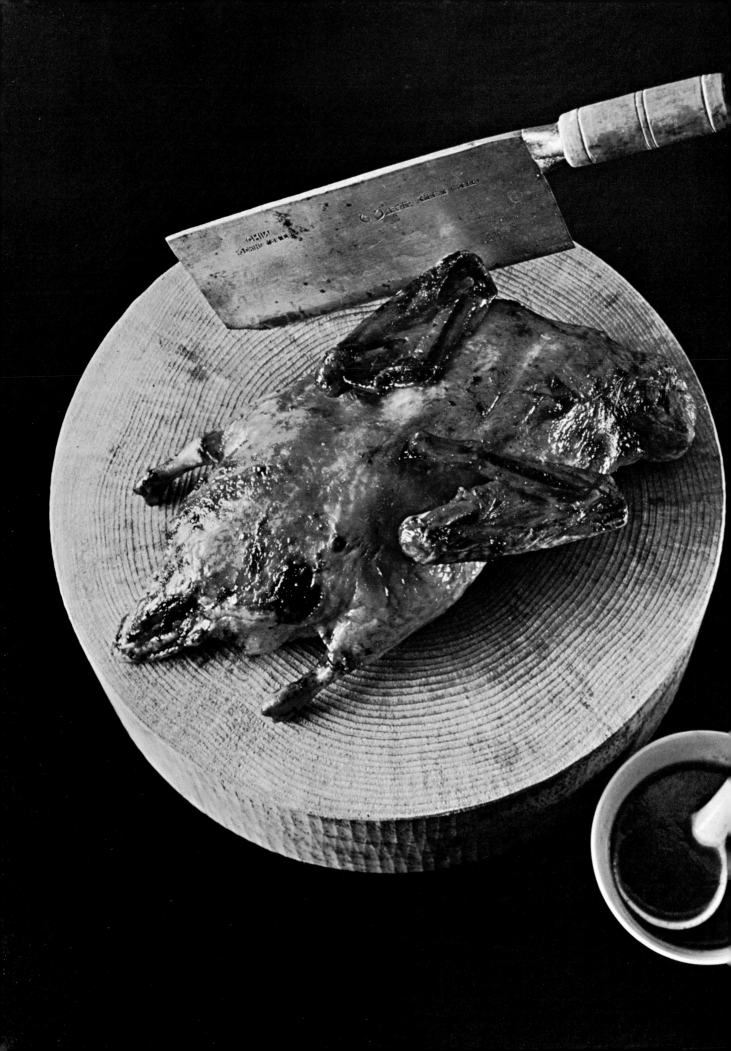

Poultry and eggs

Probably no one in the world approaches poultry with as much imagination and flare as the Chinese. And no one does as well to make ordinary boiled chicken into out-of-the-ordinary fare. Unless, of course, it's the Japanese. Here are some standouts from both cultures, and some unusual ways to cook eggs.

When I was a child, I thought there were two kinds of chicken, fried and with dumplings. And when I was a child, I was convinced that I got the wing only because I was the lowest one on the family totem pole.

So now I envy Oriental youngsters, especially Chinese ones. They grow up knowing about dozens of unusual, delectable ways with chicken, and they grow up appreciating the tender, melting succulence of the wings. (Many dishes are based on the wings alone.)

Nothing wasted

In Chinese home kitchens there is a way to cook every part of a chicken or duck. I confess that I still find chicken or duck feet strange, and at a banquet in Hong Kong I was startled to see a whole boiled chicken sitting on a plate with a kumquat in its beak. But as a lady with a budget I am delighted by this thrifty approach. And if a fish can eye me from a platter, why not a chicken?

Because it is meant to be eaten with chopsticks, poultry is usually boned or cut up into small pieces before it is cooked or before it is served. But for dishes like *teriyaki,* I prefer to use standard Western-style parts because the large pieces are easier to handle on the barbecue or in the broiler.

To bone poultry: Cut the raw meat from the bone, then cut in bite-size pieces for stir-frying or for use in recipes that follow. The easiest part to bone is the breast. When breasts

Roast Duck is special to serve at any meal —Western or Oriental. See page 72 for recipe.

are on sale, I pick up several bags for the freezer. I cut them in half, freeze them on a cookie sheet, then pack in plastic bags.

I don't worry about getting every bit of meat off because the bones go into the soup pot for stock. The skin goes into the pot, too, because chicken skins are usually fatty. You get about ½ cup chicken meat from half a medium-sized breast.

To cut up, Oriental-style: You do this before or after cooking, depending upon the recipe. Cut off the wings and legs. Divide the body in half lengthwise by cutting through the breast and backbone. Place skin side up on a board; with a cleaver, chop through the halves, bones and all, at 1-inch intervals. Cut the wings and legs into small pieces.

This takes a bit of practice. Your first whack should go clear through each time; otherwise the bone slivers.

Cashew Chicken

2 cups raw boneless chicken, cut in bite-size pieces
1 tablespoon *each* soy sauce, cornstarch, and sherry
½ teaspoon salt
1 clove garlic, minced
1 teaspoon grated ginger root
  Salad oil for cooking
¾ cup cashew nuts
½ cup sliced bamboo shoots
8 fresh mushrooms, sliced
1 stalk celery, cut diagonally in slices ⅛ inch thick
  Salt
15 edible podded peas, ends and side strings removed
¾ cup water mixed with 1 tablespoon soy sauce, 1 tablespoon cornstarch, and ½ teaspoon sugar

1. Marinate chicken for 15 minutes in soy sauce, cornstarch, sherry, salt, garlic, and ginger.

2. Heat 1 tablespoon of salad oil in a wok or frying pan over medium heat; sauté nuts until lightly browned. Remove.

3. Heat 2 tablespoons oil over high heat; add bamboo shoots, mushrooms, and celery; stir-fry for 2 minutes or until vegetables are crisp tender. Remove from pan.

4. Heat 1 tablespoon of oil over high heat, sprinkle with salt, add peas, and stir-fry 1 minute. Remove.

5. Heat 2 tablespoons of oil over high heat. Add marinated chicken and stir-fry for 4 minutes or until meat is white. Scrape bottom of pan with turner to prevent sticking. Return vegetables and nuts to pan. Stir cornstarch-water mixture to recombine it; pour in and stir and cook until thickened. Serves 4 to 6.

Jade Chicken

1 tablespoon cornstarch
2 teaspoons *each* sherry and soy sauce
¼ teaspoon monosodium glutamate
½ teaspoon *each* salt and sugar
1 clove garlic, minced
1 teaspoon grated ginger root
1½ cups raw boneless chicken, cut in bite-size pieces
  Salad oil for cooking
1 cup Thompson seedless grapes
⅓ cup water
1 teaspoon cornstarch mixed with 1 tablespoon water and ½ teaspoon sugar

1. Combine cornstarch, sherry, soy sauce, monosodium glutamate, salt, sugar, garlic, and ginger; add chicken and let stand 15 minutes.

2. Heat 2 tablespoons of oil in a wok or frying pan; add chicken and stir-fry over high heat 3 to 4 minutes or until meat is white and tender. Scrape with a turner to prevent sticking. Remove from pan.

Yakitori *and fresh soybeans are a Japanese classic. Cook beans briefly in boiling water, shell, eat like peanuts.*

glutamate in a shallow casserole or pan that will fit inside a steamer. Add chicken and mushrooms and mix with sauce. Stir in oil.

2. Place lemon slices and ginger over chicken. Steam in a steamer for 30 minutes. Serve hot. Serves 4 to 6.

Chicken Yakitori

These small skewers threaded with chicken and chicken livers are good for appetizers and snacks—even an entrée if you make enough of them.

½ cup soy sauce
½ cup sherry, *sake,* or *mirin*
3 tablespoons sugar
3 whole chicken breasts, boned, skinned, and cut in bite-size pieces
7 large green onions, cut white part of each in two 2-inch lengths
1 pound chicken livers, cut in half
6 water chestnuts, cut in half

1. To make basting sauce, cook soy sauce, sherry, and sugar for 3 minutes.

2. Using 6-inch bamboo or metal skewers, thread 6 pieces chicken breast and 2 lengths green onion alternately on 14 skewers. Thread 6 pieces chicken liver and 2 slices of water chestnut alternately on 6 additional skewers. Dip skewers in basting sauce so all the meat is coated.

3. Broil 5 to 7 inches from the heat for 10 minutes or until meat is tender. Brush with basting sauce and turn occasionally during cooking. Makes 20 skewers.

Mizutaki—Japanese Boiled Chicken

This is not a traditional version—it is mine. The Japanese don't bone the meat, and often cook *mizutaki* at the table; I bone the meat, cook everything in the kitchen, and serve it in individual bowls. We pour the broth that is left in each bowl over rice, along with a few drops of the dipping sauce.

1 small Chinese cabbage (about 1½ pounds)
2 whole chicken breasts, boned and cut in 2-inch pieces
6 cups water
2 teaspoons salt
⅛ teaspoon monosodium glutamate
4 dried mushrooms, presoaked and thinly sliced
1 square *tofu* (cut in small cubes)
¼ cup lemon juice
½ cup *each* soy sauce and chicken stock
3 green onions and tops, finely chopped

1. Cut cabbage in 2-inch squares, separating the thick part of the stem from the tender leaves.

2. Place chicken and water in a

3. Heat 1 tablespoon oil over high heat. Add grapes and stir-fry 1 minute. Add water and cook 30 seconds. Add chicken. Stir cornstarch-water mixture to recombine it; pour in, stir, and cook until thickened.
Serves 3 to 4.

Paper-Wrapped Chicken

You can use foil for wrapping instead of paper and cook the same length of time. Chicken in foil steams rather than browns but the flavor is still good. I wrap in foil when I want to cook over a barbecue.

2 Chinese sausages (optional)
2 whole chicken breasts, boned, skinned, and cut in bite-size pieces
1 tablespoon *each* soy sauce, sherry, *hoisin* sauce, and Worcestershire
1 tablespoon cornstarch
1 teaspoon sesame oil
1 clove garlic, minced
1 green onion and top, finely chopped
½ teaspoon salt
2 tablespoons salad oil

1. Steam sausages for 15 minutes; cut diagonally in slices ⅛ inch thick. Marinate chicken for 30 minutes in mixture of the remaining ingredients.

2. Cut parchment paper or waxed paper into 3 dozen 4-inch squares.

Place 2 teaspoons chicken and one slice Chinese sausage in the middle of a square. Think of the square as a baseball diamond. Fold home plate almost to second base; fold first and third bases into the pitcher's mound. Turn the top corner of the paper (second base) down as you would to close an envelope and fit into the slit made by the folds in the paper.

3. Arrange packets in a single layer on a cookie sheet. Cover loosely with aluminum foil. Bake in a hot oven (400°) for 8 minutes. Remove foil and continue baking for 8 minutes. The packets should become slightly tan without burning. Serve chicken, still in its wrapper, so each person can unfold and munch. Makes 36.

Lemon Chicken

1 tablespoon *each* soy sauce, cornstarch, and oyster sauce
1 teaspoon salt
¼ teaspoon monosodium glutamate
2 chicken breasts, boned, skinned, and cut in 1-inch pieces
6 dried mushrooms, presoaked and thinly sliced
2 tablespoons salad oil
1 lemon, thinly sliced
2 thin slices ginger root, cut in slivers

1. Place soy sauce, cornstarch, oyster sauce, salt, and monosodium

pan and boil for 10 minutes; skim off foam. Add salt, monosodium glutamate, thicker cabbage stems, and mushrooms to chicken and simmer for 10 minutes. Add the tender part of leaves and *tofu* and simmer for 15 minutes.

3. Combine lemon juice, soy sauce, and chicken stock for dipping sauce. Pour into 6 individual sauce bowls and mix green onions into the sauce.

4. Ladle some of the chicken, cabbage, *tofu,* and broth into individual bowls. To eat, dip each item into the onion-flavored sauce. Serves 6.

Chicken Wings with Oyster Sauce

2 pounds chicken wings
1 teaspoon salt
1 tablespoon sherry or rice wine
3 tablespoons salad oil
1 tablespoon soy sauce
1 bunch green onions, cut in 1½-inch lengths and shredded
2 tablespoons *each* oyster sauce and water

1. Cut chicken wings between joints; save tips for soup or stock. Marinate wing pieces for 1 hour in salt, sherry, 1 tablespoon of the oil, soy sauce, and green onions. Remove from marinade, scraping off as much of the green onion as you can. Save marinade and onion.

2. Heat the remaining 2 tablespoons oil in a large frying pan. Add wings and brown well on all sides. Add oyster sauce, water, and remaining marinade and onions. Cover and simmer for 15 minutes or until tender. Serves 6.

Chicken Teriyaki

Split 2 broiler-fryer chickens in half lengthwise, wash, and pat dry with paper toweling. Place in a plastic bag and add *Teriyaki* Sauce (see page 67). Close bag tightly and marinate overnight.

Remove chicken from marinade and place on a rack in a baking pan, skin side up. Bake in a moderately slow oven (300°) for 45 minutes. Turn over, brush with marinade, and bake 15 minutes. Turn again so the skin side is up, brush with marinade and continue baking for 15 minutes. Cut chicken Oriental or Western style. Serve hot or at room temperature. Serves 8.

For a quick version, cut 1 chicken into serving-size pieces. Heat 2 tablespoons salad oil in frying pan and brown chicken on all sides. Pour off excess oil. Add ½ cup *Teriyaki* Sauce and 2 tablespoons water. Cover and simmer 45 minutes.

Korean Chicken with Cellophane Noodles

1 broiler-fryer chicken, cut in serving-size pieces
3 tablespoons soy sauce
2 cloves garlic, minced
½ teaspoon *each* salt, monosodium glutamate, and pepper
Dash of cayenne
2 teaspoons crushed toasted sesame seeds
2 tablespoons salad oil
4 dried mushrooms, presoaked and thinly sliced (save ½ cup of soaking liquid)
¾ cup water
1 onion, cut in 8 wedges
2 stalks celery, cut diagonally in ½-inch lengths
1 bundle (4 oz.) cellophane noodles, presoaked 30 minutes and cut in 4-inch lengths
4 green onions and tops, cut in 1-inch lengths

1. Marinate chicken for 30 minutes in soy sauce, garlic, salt, monosodium glutamate, pepper, cayenne, and sesame seeds.

2. Heat the 2 tablespoons oil in a frying pan; remove chicken from marinade, drain, and brown slowly on all sides. Add remaining marinade, mushrooms, mushroom liquid, water, onion, and celery to browned chicken. Cover and simmer for 40 minutes.

3. Add drained cellophane noodles to pan and cook for 10 minutes. Sprinkle green onions over the top and stir in just before serving. Serves 4 to 6.

Peanut-Flavored Chicken Teriyaki

¼ cup *each* peanut butter, soy sauce, and sherry
2 tablespoons sugar
½ teaspoon grated ginger root
⅛ teaspoon monosodium glutamate
1 broiler-fryer chicken, cut in serving-size pieces

1. Mix together the peanut butter, soy sauce, sherry, sugar, ginger, and monosodium glutamate until smooth. Pour over chicken pieces and marinate for 1 hour.

2. Place chicken on a rack set in a baking pan. Bake in a moderate oven (350°) for 1 hour. Brush with marinade twice during baking. Serves 4.

Velvet Chicken with Green Onion Relish

This is a super-simple recipe—one that does not require last-minute timing. The chicken is smooth and juicy, a good contrast to the spicy relishes. It is meant to be eaten slightly warm or at room temperature; refrigeration does something to the velvety texture, making it taste like ordinary boiled chicken.

The soup broth is an extra bonus. I often make soup out of it for the same meal. Be sure not to overcook the chicken.

1 onion, cut in quarters
2 teaspoons salt
14 cups water
1 whole broiler-fryer chicken
3 tablespoons salad oil
1 tablespoon dry mustard
1 teaspoon water
2 tablespoons soy sauce
3 green onions and tops, cut in 1½-inch lengths and shredded
½ teaspoon salt

1. Place onion, salt, and water in an 8-quart kettle and bring to a boil. Add the whole chicken, bring to a boil again, and immediately lower heat. Simmer, covered, for 40 minutes. Turn off heat and let stand 15 minutes.

2. Lift chicken out of stock with a spoon and cool slightly. Strain stock and save for soup. Rub 1 tablespoon of the oil over chicken. Cut in 2-inch pieces, cutting through the bone, or cut chicken off the bone in large pieces and then cut in bite-size pieces.

3. Mix mustard and water; combine with soy sauce and another tablespoon of the oil. Place in a small bowl. Toss green onions and tops with the ½ teaspoon salt and the remaining tablespoon oil. Place in another small bowl.

4. Arrange chicken on a platter. Pass relishes as dipping sauces for chicken. Serves 6.

Sesame Pineapple Chicken

This has a delicious, sweet spicy sauce. It's a good choice for hot days —easy cooking and refreshing flavor.

1 whole broiler-fryer chicken, cooked according to the directions in the previous recipe Velvet Chicken
1 flat can (8 oz.) sliced pineapple
½ cup plum sauce
2 tablespoons sugar
1 tablespoon vinegar
3 tablespoons toasted sesame seeds
Shredded green onions and Chinese parsley for garnish

1. Cool chicken and cut into serving-size pieces, with or without the bone. Arrange on a platter.

2. Drain pineapple, save juice, and cut each slice into small wedges. Mix together the pineapple juice, plum sauce, sugar, vinegar, and sesame seeds until smooth; stir in pineapple. Pour sauce over chicken and garnish with green onion and Chinese parsley. Serve cold. Serves 6.

Dangling roast ducks are a familiar sight in Chinese markets. Buy a half or whole one; reheat briefly in oven.

Roast Duck

This takes a combination of techniques. Hanging the duck to dry and pumping up the stomach cavity makes the skin crisp. Pouring the liquid inside the duck gives it a savory flavor.

1 duck (4 to 5 pounds)
2 tablespoons *hoisin* sauce
1 tablespoon brown bean sauce
3 tablespoons soy sauce
1 tablespoon rice wine or sherry
2 tablespoons sugar
2 teaspoons salt
1 cup warm water
1 green onion and top finely chopped
¼ cup honey
**   *Hoisin* sauce or plum sauce**
**   Chinese parsley**

1. If duck is frozen, defrost overnight in refrigerator. Wash and pat dry with paper toweling, both inside and out. Tie a string around the flap of skin at the neck opening and hang bird in a cool place for 3 hours or until the skin is taut and dry. If you have an electric fan, you can dry the duck in 2 hours.

2. Sew up neck cavity, overlapping the skin and sewing tightly. Sew the stomach cavity, leaving a small opening. Place the duck, neck down, in a pan or bowl. Mix the *hoisin* sauce, brown bean sauce, soy sauce, rice wine or sherry, sugar, salt, water, and green onion. Pour into stomach cavity, then finish sewing the cavity. If you have sewn the duck tightly the liquid will not leak out.

3. Screw an inflating needle in a bicycle pump, insert the needle into the stomach cavity (between the stitches) and pump. This gives a fullness to the stomach area which shrinks in the drying stage. Don't worry, the duck won't burst. After it is filled with air, the extra air leaks out.

4. Place duck on a rack in a roasting pan breast side up. Roast in a hot oven (400°) for 50 minutes. Brush honey over duck and continue roasting for 10 minutes. Carefully turn duck over, brush honey on the back, and continue roasting for 15 minutes or until duck is tender.

5. Remove duck from oven and transfer to another pan; discard drippings. Cut strings and let the juices from the cavity drain into pan. Transfer duck to a cutting board and cut in serving-size pieces. Reheat juices and serve along with *hoisin* sauce or plum sauce and Chinese parsley. Serves 6 to 8.

Tea-Smoked Duck

You might guess it would take hours to smoke a duck, but it can be done easily in your kitchen in 5 minutes. In restaurants the smoked duck is fried in deep fat for the final crisping. Because there is so much splattering and spewing, I find it much easier to do the final crisping in the oven.

1 duck, about 5 pounds
2 tablespoons sherry
1 teaspoon salt
3 green onions and tops, cut in
**   1½-inch lengths**
10 thin slices ginger root
1 teaspoon whole Szechwan peppercorns, crushed with a cleaver
2 tablespoons *each* black tea leaves and uncooked rice
**   Mandarin pancakes (see page 65)**
**   *Hoisin* sauce or plum sauce**

1. Wash and dry duck. In a bowl, combine sherry, salt, green onions, ginger, and peppercorns. With your hands, rub duck inside and out with the mixture, pressing onion and ginger against the skin and inside the cavity of the duck. Cover and refrigerate overnight.

2. Place duck, breast side up, on a plate or in a shallow bowl and steam for 1 hour. Remove from steamer; pour off and discard drippings. Steaming tenderizes the duck and eliminates a great deal of the fat. Chill duck, then cut in half lengthwise.

3. In the bottom of a wok, place the tea leaves and rice. Place a rack, such as a round wire cake rack, over the tea-rice mixture. Place duck halves on the rack. Cover with a wok lid or a large mixing bowl turned upside down. Turn on heat to high for 2 minutes. Turn off heat and let stand 5 minutes. Don't peek. You must wait for the smoke to subside. When you lift the lid you will no longer see the ivory-colored duck—it will be coppery bronze. Don't worry about pan and lid. They will wash easily.

4. Cut duck through the bone into serving size pieces. Cover and refrigerate for as long as three days. When you want to serve, place duck pieces on a rack in a roasting pan. Bake in a moderate oven (350°) for

Duck shrinks as it hangs and dries. This makes skin crisp after roasting.

Duck becomes plump and fat again when you pump it up. Use inflating needle.

Complement crispy skin and succulent meat of roast duck with hoisin sauce.

To make Japanese omelet, roll egg layer toward you gently so it encloses sheet of nori.

Sliced omelet is good for breakfast, lunch, hors d'oeuvre. Garnish with umeboshi *(salted plum).*

30 minutes for the duck to reheat and become crisp. Serve with Mandarin pancakes if you wish and pass a bowl of *hoisin* or plum sauce to dip the crispy meat in. Serves 6 to 8.

Chawan Mushi—Steamed Custard

My introduction to *chawan mushi* came with my first invitation to a Japanese home for lunch. Mrs. Hourami had planned the menu to fit the season. It was a cold wintry day, and I welcomed this savory hot custard—which she served in place of a soup—as well as the small heater placed near my slippered feet.

3 cups *dashi* (see page 33) or chicken stock
1 cup well beaten eggs
1 teaspoon *each* salt and sugar
 Dash of monosodium glutamate
1 teaspoon soy sauce
¾ cup diced raw chicken or raw peeled shrimp
2 mushrooms, sliced
½ cup green vegetables (peas, edible podded peas, cut asparagus, or green beans), cooked lightly and drained
 Lemon peel for garnish

1. Combine *dashi* or chicken stock with eggs; strain through a sieve, then mix in the salt, sugar, monosodium glutamate, and soy sauce.

2. Distribute equal portions of chicken or shrimp, mushroom slices, and vegetables in 6 *chawan mushi* cups with lids or custard cups. Pour egg mixture into the cups. Cover cups with lids or aluminum foil. Steam for 15 to 20 minutes, or set covered cups in a baking pan, pour hot water nearly to the top of the cups, and bake in a moderate oven (350°) for 35 to 40 minutes. The custard should be set but will retain a little liquid which drains from the vegetables during cooking. Serve hot and eat with a spoon. Serves 6.

Scrambled Eggs with Cellophane Noodles

4 eggs
½ teaspoon salt
1 teaspoon soy sauce
1 ounce cellophane noodles, soaked for 30 minutes, drained, and cut in 1-inch lengths
2 green onions and tops, finely chopped
¼ cup diced barbecued pork or cooked ham
1 tablespoon salad oil

1. Beat eggs slightly with salt and soy sauce. Stir in cellophane noodles, onions, and barbecued pork.

2. Heat oil in a frying pan over medium heat. Pour in egg mixture and cook until eggs set. Serves 3.

Japanese Rolled Omelet

A rectangular frying pan makes it easy to cook this omelet in a uniform roll, but a frying pan with a nonstick surface will work as well.

3 large eggs, well beaten
⅓ cup *dashi* (page 33) or chicken stock
½ teaspoon soy sauce
¼ teaspoon salt
 Dash of monosodium glutamate
 ***Nori* (laver seaweed)**
 Sesame oil

1. Combine eggs, *dashi,* soy sauce, salt, and monosodium glutamate.

2. Toast *nori* by passing it briefly over a flame or over an electric burner turned to high. If you use *yaki nori,* it is not necessary to toast it. Cut 2 pieces of *nori* to fit the length of the frying pan. Cut 2 more pieces to fit three-fourths the length of pan.

3. Brush a thin film of sesame oil over pan. Heat pan over medium heat until a drop of water on the surface sizzles. Pour in enough egg mixture to coat pan lightly. Tip pan back and forth over heat until egg begins to set. Cover with one of the larger pieces of *nori.* Cook for 30

seconds. Remove pan from heat. Starting at the end away from you, loosen edge of egg with a chopstick or wooden spatula, lift up, and roll toward you like a jelly roll.

4. Slide the rolled omelet to the far end of the pan. Return pan to heat. Brush lightly with oil. Pour in egg mixture to coat pan lightly, letting some of it run under the first completed omelet. When egg begins to set, cover with a shorter piece of *nori* and cook another 30 seconds. Roll again toward you, starting with the completed omelet and enclosing the new egg as you roll. Lift out of pan and make a second omelet.

5. Cool slightly, cut each roll in 1-inch-thick slices. Makes 2 rolls when cooked in a 5x8-inch pan.

Foo Yung—Chinese Omelet

6 eggs, lightly beaten
1 cup flaked crab meat
1 teaspoon sherry or rice wine
½ teaspoon salt
3 tablespoons salad oil
2 dried mushrooms, presoaked and thinly sliced
¼ cup *each* frozen peas (thawed) and shredded bamboo shoots
1 cup chicken stock
2 teaspoons soy sauce
1 teaspoon sugar
2 teaspoons cornstarch mixed with 1 tablespoon water

1. Combine eggs, crab, wine, and salt. Heat 2 tablespoons of the oil in a pan over medium high heat. Add egg mixture, cook until half set, and turn to fry the other side. Remove.

2. Sauté mushrooms, peas, and bamboo shoots in remaining 1 tablespoon oil for 1 minute. Add chicken stock, soy sauce, and sugar; simmer 1 minute. Add cornstarch-water mixture and cook until sauce is slightly thickened. Pour over eggs. Serves 3 to 4.

Fish and shellfish

The Japanese are as creative with fish as the Chinese are with chicken. This isn't from overabundance, but from necessity. Neither culture allows anything to go to waste. "Less is more," as someone once said. You'll find this true when you try fish in Oriental ways.

In Japan, I shopped weekly at the wholesale fish market. Part of me was there as an adventurous and curious and communicative cook; part a thrifty shopper; and part was a wide-eyed tourist, agape at the spread of colors, shapes, textures, and varieties such as I'd never seen before—all with little notion of how to make peace with them over a hot stove.

Make peace I did, eventually, but I can make no attempt, here, to share the fish specifics. I cannot bring back the fish; I can only bring back the methods.

Fresh fish shopping

These days, whenever possible, I shop for fish in San Francisco's Chinatown, Japantown, or Fisherman's Wharf, just for the sake of getting fresh fish. Sometimes in Chinatown the fish are still swimming when I choose them. Whenever I can, I make it clear to the fishermen in my family or any fishermen we know that I will be forever beholden to them if they remember my fresh-fish yearnings from time to time.

In the following recipes, I use the freshest possible fish that I can get. Sometimes the freshest possible fish is frozen. It's the cooking method and the surprising seasonings that make each dish and each fish special.

Oriental Steamed Fish

Both the Chinese and the Japanese like to cook fish whole. Sometimes my own fishermen or our friends bring small whole fish in: black bass,

◁

Fish, fresh from the market or sportsman's line, are delicious steamed the Oriental way.

trout, perch, flounder. Otherwise, I buy kingfish, sand dabs, or small red snappers. You can apply this recipe to larger fish, too; I usually don't because they look less attractive cut up into pieces.

1 fresh or saltwater fish, 2 to 2½ pounds or 2 smaller fish
Salt
1 tablespoon sherry
2 tablespoons soy sauce
½ teaspoon sugar
½ teaspoon salt
2 teaspoons vinegar
1 teaspoon salad oil
2 slices ginger root, minced
4 dried mushrooms, presoaked
2 green onions

1. To prepare fish, clean, scale, rinse; pat dry with paper toweling. Rub lightly inside and out with salt. Place in shallow bowl that will fit your steamer.

2. Mix together sherry, soy sauce, sugar, salt, vinegar, salad oil, and ginger root. Pour over fish. Place mushrooms on fish.

3. Place fish in steamer. Steam until fish flakes with a fork (6 to 8 minutes for a flat fish, 12 minutes for a 1½-pound one, 20 minutes for 2½-pound one).

4. Cut green onions in 2-inch lengths; shred. Distribute on fish 2 minutes before serving. Serves 4.

Stir-Fried Fish with Vegetables

This is a really fast way to cook a whole family meal at once—fish and vegetables, served with rice. It came from a lady named Ayako, who is married to a man named Kim; it's a maverick meal, but it's delicious. Don't be tempted to add more soy sauce, because it will overpower the seasonings and muddy the color.

Salad oil for frying
1 small onion, cut in half lengthwise, then cut in ¼-inch-thick slices
1 large stalk celery, cut diagonally in slices ⅛ inch thick
5 water chestnuts, sliced ⅛ inch thick
½ cup sliced bamboo shoots
8 fresh mushrooms, sliced ¼ inch thick
½ teaspoon salt
1 pound white fish fillets (rock fish, sea bass, or any firm white fish), cut crosswise in slices ¼ inch thick
1 teaspoon minced ginger root
1 teaspoon salt
2 teaspoons sherry or rice wine
1 teaspoon soy sauce
2 teaspoons cornstarch mixed with 1 tablespoon water

1. Heat 2 tablespoons oil in a wok or frying pan over high heat. Add onion, celery, water chestnuts, bamboo shoots, and mushrooms; stir-fry for 2 minutes. Sprinkle with the ½ teaspoon salt, stir once, and cover pan for 1 minute. Remove from pan.

2. Heat 3 tablespoons oil in wok. Add fish, ginger, and the 1 teaspoon salt. Stir-fry until fish turns white, about 2 minutes. Turn fish over carefully as you stir so it will not break apart. Add sherry and soy sauce.

3. Return vegetables to the pan. Stir cornstarch-water mixture to recombine, add to pan, and cook, stirring until sauce is slightly thickened, about 30 seconds. Serves 4 to 6.

Poached Fish in Shoyu

The first time I ate this in Japan, the fish was "in the round," head, tail, and all, and I do it that way whenever I find sand dabs or other small flat fish. I score the top lightly and poach it briefly.

In Japan, to make the fish look as if it were in motion, it was served in a too-small bowl, so the head and tail curved upward. For my family—in too much of a hurry to appreciate moving fish—I use fillets, flat. It's not as artistic, but it tastes as good.

    1 cup water
    ½ cup soy sauce
    ¼ cup sugar
    2 tablespoons *mirin* or sherry
    1 teaspoon grated ginger root
        Dash monosodium glutamate
    6 small pieces fillet of sole, cut in half
        crosswise
    18 green onions, wash, trim and cut off
        the tops so onions measure 3 inches

1. Boil water, soy sauce, sugar, *mirin,* ginger, and monosodium glutamate in a large frying pan for 2 minutes. Reduce heat and add fish. Simmer for 5 to 7 minutes or until fish flakes with a fork. Arrange fish in 6 small bowls, two pieces in each bowl.

2. Place green onions in pan and poach in the sauce for 2 minutes. Garnish each serving with three green onions. Pour 2 tablespoons sauce over each serving. Serves 6.

Chef Chu's Dragon Fish

This is one restaurant specialty that I enjoy serving to guests at home. The cutting is easy and can be done early in the day. In restaurants, the fish is deep fried in a wok, but I prefer to cook mine in a flat-bottom heavy kettle so there won't be any chance of the pan tipping over.

    ¾ cup chicken stock
    ½ cup sugar
    ½ cup vinegar
    1 tablespoon soy sauce
    2 tablespoons catsup
    ½ cup Chinese pickled mixed vegeta-
        bles, or pickled ginger, shredded,
        plus 2 tablespoons pickling syrup.
    2 tablespoons cornstarch mixed with
        3 tablespoons water
    1 3 to 4 pound red snapper

1. In a pan, combine chicken stock, sugar, vinegar, soy sauce, catsup, pickled vegetables, and pickling syrup. Heat to boiling. Stir cornstarch-water mixture, add to pan, and stirring, cook until sauce thickens.

2. Prepare fish according to illustration. Hold fish by the tail and dip in hot water. This "shrinks" the meat and accents the diamond pattern. Coat fish with flour.

3. Pour oil in a large kettle so it is 4 inches deep. Heat to 350°. Hold fish so skin sides are back to back. Grasping both ends, slowly immerse in hot oil. Cook until golden brown, about 5 minutes. Remove fish, drain, and place on a platter. Cook the unfloured fish head in hot oil for 3 minutes; drain. Arrange fish head at top of fish. Reheat sauce and spoon over fish before serving. Serves 4 to 6.

Preparing the dragon fish

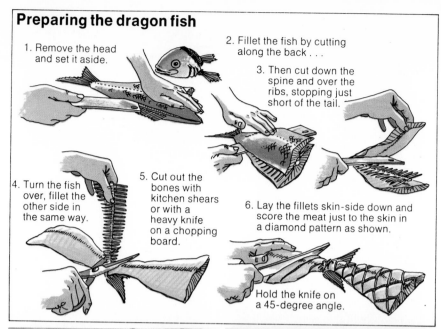

1. Remove the head and set it aside.

2. Fillet the fish by cutting along the back . . .

3. Then cut down the spine and over the ribs, stopping just short of the tail.

4. Turn the fish over, fillet the other side in the same way.

5. Cut out the bones with kitchen shears or with a heavy knife on a chopping board.

6. Lay the fillets skin-side down and score the meat just to the skin in a diamond pattern as shown.

Hold the knife on a 45-degree angle.

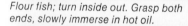
Flour fish; turn inside out. Grasp both ends, slowly immerse in hot oil.

Lift cooked fish from oil with wire strainer. Fish head is cooked too.

Dragon fish makes an imaginative entrée for a very special occasion. Serve with sweet-sour sauce.

Salmon Miso-Yaki

This is also very delicious barbecued. Use very low coals, because the sauce burns easily.

½ cup white *miso* (soybean paste)
1 tablespoon *each* soy sauce, sugar, and sherry
Dash monosodium glutamate
1 pound salmon fillets or steaks

1. Blend *miso* with soy sauce, sugar, sherry, and monosodium glutamate. Spread on both sides of salmon and refrigerate for 24 hours.

2. Place fish on a rack in a broiling pan, leaving a thick layer of *miso* sauce on both sides. Broil 5 to 7 inches from the heat, about 4 minutes on each side, depending on the thickness of the fish. Serves 4.

Fish Baked in Foil

4 fish fillets or steaks of salmon, halibut, or sea bass, *or* 4 whole trout
Salt and pepper
½ small onion, thinly sliced and rings separated
4 thin slices lemon
2 tablespoons *sake* or sherry

1. Sprinkle fish with salt and pepper and let stand 5 minutes. Cut 4 pieces of aluminum foil twice the size of the fish and place fish in the center of each.

2. Top each with a few onion rings and a lemon slice. Sprinkle with *sake* and seal foil tightly. Place in a baking pan. Bake in a moderate oven (350°) for 15 to 20 minutes, depending on thickness of fish. Serve in the foil packets. Serves 4.

Stuffed Fish with Egg Yolk Glaze

Occasionally I can find fresh quail eggs in Chinatown or can get them from 4-H youngsters, but they're almost as good canned. Fillets are not thick enough for this; I buy sea bass or halibut steaks cut a little over 1 inch thick. I split the steaks, remove the skin and bones, and end up with 6 pieces just the right size.

6 boneless slices of white fish, 3 inches long, 2 inches wide, and 1 inch thick
Salt and white pepper
2 green onions and part of tops, finely chopped
12 hard-boiled quail eggs
2 egg yolks
Dash *each* salt and monosodium glutamate
1 teaspoon *mirin* or sherry
6 pickled ginger sprouts for garnish

1. Cut a pocket in the side of each fish slice. Sprinkle inside of pockets lightly with salt, pepper, and green onion. Stuff 2 quail eggs into each fish slice. Place on a lightly greased baking pan.

The Japanese approach combines flavor and a picture-like quality in this fish stuffed with quail eggs.

2. Beat egg yolks with salt, monosodium glutamate, and *mirin*. Brush over top of fish slices. Bake in a moderate oven (350°) until you can pierce the edge of the fish easily with a fork, about 10 to 12 minutes. Brush egg yolk mixture over fish twice during baking. Garnish with pickled ginger sprouts. Serves 6.

Fish Teriyaki

Prepare Basic Teriyaki Sauce (see page 67). Marinate 2 pounds fish fillets or steaks—salmon, sea bass, red snapper, tuna, or ling cod—in sauce for 2 hours.

Remove fillets from marinade and place on a rack set in a baking pan. Broil 5 to 7 inches from the heat, about 3 to 4 minutes on each side. Test with a fork to see if the fish flakes easily. Thick pieces of fish may take a few minutes longer, but do not overcook. Baste with marinade several times during cooking. Serve with a little heated marinade.

Sashimi

The Japanese serve many different kinds of fish and shellfish as *sashimi*. I've dipped raw scallops, abalone, and squid into lemon juice and soy sauce and enjoyed their unique flavors and textures. My favorites for *sashimi,* however, are tuna, sea bass, and striped bass. For guests I serve *sashimi* as an appetizer. On a hot day, it's one of the easiest dinners I can prepare for my family.

Fresh fish and a sharp knife

There are two rules for preparing *sashimi.* You must begin with very fresh fish and must cut it with a very sharp knife to obtain the desired glaze on each slice. I buy the fish at a Japanese market that sells fillet of bass and tuna. Unless they have a Japanese clientele, most fish markets cut their fish into steaks—good for barbecuing but not for *sashimi.*

Fresh tuna. Sometimes when you buy tuna, it's pink; another time it's a darker red. The difference is in the variety of tuna and where it was caught. It's all good. The best part for *sashimi* is the back center fillet—the meat becomes stringy near the tail. Some people prefer the flavor of the meat near the stomach; it is a little more fatty. After you buy the fillet, remove and discard the skin and very dark parts of the meat. Cut the fillet in 2-inch lengths, then cut across the grain in slices ¼ inch thick, and 1 inch wide.

Sea bass. The size of the fillet determines the shape of the pieces. Traditionally, tuna is cut into domino-shaped pieces. Sea bass, which is firmer in texture, can be cut in much thinner slices. You can also cut sea bass in cubes and if your piece tapers at one end, there is nothing wrong with a diamond-shaped piece.

Striped bass. This game fish is not sold commercially but makes excellent *sashimi* if you can get it. Cover the fillet and refrigerate for one

Fresh tuna is a favorite fish to serve as sashimi. *Dip each slice in soy sauce blended with* wasabi *(Japanese horseradish). The shreds of* daikon *are meant to be eaten too.*

night. The fish "relaxes" with one-day's standing and gains a better texture. Cut into domino-shaped pieces.

It is best to buy just the amount of fish for *sashimi* that you think you will use at one time. If you overbuy (which I occasionally do), slice what you think will be eaten at one time. Cover the remainder with plastic film and refrigerate.

Sashimi garnishes

Daikon is the traditional garnish for *sashimi*. Shred with the fine blade of the Japanese grater (see page 58) and let stand in cold water for 30 minutes. Mix *wasabi* (Japanese horseradish) with a little water until it is the consistency of sour cream. *Wasabi* is hot and a little goes a long way. Give each person a small dipping bowl of soy sauce. To eat, mix ½ teaspoon (or more) *wasabi* with the soy sauce, dip in the *sashimi*, snitch a bit of shredded *daikon*, and enjoy.

Clams and other seafood

Here are two ways with clams, just to point out the differences in the Japanese and Chinese approach. In the Japanese version, the flavor taps you on the back and shyly whispers, "I'm a clam, do you like me?" In the Chinese version the flavor jumps up, shakes your hand, and boldly proclaims, "I'm a clam and proud of it." Either way, my family downs them by the dozen.

Japanese Steamed Clams

4 thin slices ginger root
3 tablespoons soy sauce
1 tablespoon sugar
¼ cup water
2 dozen small clams in the shell, washed and drained

1. Place ginger, soy sauce, sugar, and water in a large kettle or frying pan and bring to a boil.

2. Add clams, cover, and steam over low heat until the shells open, about 10 minutes. Serve with the pan liquid for dipping. Serves 4.

Chinese Clams in Black Bean Sauce

2 teaspoons fermented black beans
1 clove garlic
2 tablespoons salad oil
¼ teaspoon salt
2 dozen small clams in the shell, washed and drained

1. Place beans in a sieve and rinse with water; mince together with garlic.

2. Heat oil in a frying pan over medium heat. Add salt and the garlic-bean mixture. Cook for 30 seconds.

3. Add clams and stir until they are coated with seasonings. Cover pan and cook over low heat for 8 to 10 minutes or until clam shells open. Serves 4.

Creamy Scallops over Vegetables

Don't expect the sauce for this dish to be like a typical cream sauce. It is delicately flavored and thin, so it complements rather than competes with the vegetables. It would also be good with finger-length pieces of zucchini, Chinese cabbage, or any bright green vegetable—as long as it is still bright green after cooking.

1½ pounds broccoli *or* asparagus
1 tablespoon salad oil
½ pound scallops *or* 1 cup canned abalone, cut in slices ⅛ inch thick
½ cup sliced bamboo shoots
1 cup chicken or pork soup stock
1 cup milk
1 teaspoon *sake* or sherry
½ teaspoon salt
Dash of monosodium glutamate
2 tablespoons cornstarch mixed with 2 tablespoons water

1. Cut broccoli in 2-inch lengths; split flowers and stems lengthwise so they will cook quickly. Or bend each stalk of asparagus until it breaks; discard tough ends. Slice diagonally or roll-cut. Cook either broccoli or asparagus in boiling water for 4 minutes; drain.

2. Heat oil in a saucepan. Sauté scallops or abalone and bamboo shoots over medium heat for 2 minutes. Add stock (if you use abalone include the liquid from the can as part of the stock measurement), and cook for 1 minute. Add milk, *sake*, salt, and monosodium glutamate and cook until heated. Stir cornstarch-water mixture, add to pan, and stir and cook until slightly thickened, about 1 minute.

3. Arrange the hot vegetables in a serving dish and pour creamy sauce over all. Serves 4.

Crab with Tofu

I don't know how an Oriental would eat this—it doesn't take to chopsticks. Because the sauce is only slightly thickened we like to spoon it over rice.

1 cup crab meat
1 teaspoon grated ginger root
2 teaspoons *sake* or sherry
1 tablespoon salad oil
2 green onions and tops, finely chopped
1 cup chicken stock or water
¼ teaspoon salt
Dash monosodium glutamate
1 square *tofu*, cut in 1-inch cubes and drained in colander
1 tablespoon cornstarch mixed with 1 tablespoon water

1. Sprinkle crab meat with ginger and *sake;* let stand 30 minutes.

2. Heat oil in a large frying pan over medium heat. Add green onions and sauté lightly. Add crab and cook 2 minutes.

3. Pour in chicken stock and season with salt and monosodium glutamate. Add *tofu*, stir gently, and cook for 3 minutes. Stir cornstarch-water mixture; add to crab, and stir and cook until slightly thickened, about 1 minute. Serves 4 to 6.

Dry Braised Prawns

I was impressed the first time I saw a friend from Taiwan pick up an unshelled prawn with chopsticks, eat the meat, and daintily deposit the shell back on her plate. It doesn't work for me; I use my fingers. Cooking the prawns in their shell seals the juices in, but for the sake of daintier eating I sometimes shell the prawns first, cook them this way, then at the last minute stir in 3 tablespoons catsup along with the sherry and soy sauce. Either way, they should be served hot.

1 pound uncooked prawns in the shell
3 tablespoons salad oil
½ teaspoon salt
1 clove garlic, minced
1 teaspoon minced ginger root
2 tablespoons sherry or rice wine
1 tablespoon soy sauce
3 green onions and tops, finely chopped

1. Wash prawns and pat dry with paper toweling. Cut through back of shell to remove sand vein (or leave it in if you wish).

2. Heat oil in wok or frying pan over high heat. Sprinkle with salt. Add prawns and stir-fry for 2 minutes. Add garlic and ginger, and cook 1 minute. Add sherry and soy sauce; stir for 30 seconds. Add green onions and cook for 30 seconds. Serve hot. Serves 4 to 5.

Tempura

When I think of *tempura*, I picture shrimp coated with a crisp, lacy covering, piping hot and succulent. When my Japanese friends think of *tempura*, they visualize fresh vegetables dipped into batter and deep-fried. We're both right: *Tempura* means to fry in deep fat.

Tempura should be eaten the instant it's cooked, so I prefer to serve it to my family or friends who don't mind eating in the kitchen. I cook everything on the stove, pass it to the table in a paper-lined basket, and replenish the basket when it comes back. This is one time when the cook eats last.

Shrimp for tempura

Shell large raw shrimp, leaving the tail for a handle. Make 2 short cuts on the inner curve. Cut along outer curve, cutting down ⅔ of the way. Spread shrimp open, so they lie flat. Wash and pat dry.

Vegetables for tempura

The possibilities are almost endless. These are some of our favorites: thin slices of sweet potato, white potato, zucchini, and Oriental eggplant, matchstick pieces of carrot, *shungiku* leaves, pencil-thin asparagus, cut in 3-inch lengths(if you use fat asparagus split in half lengthwise), large green beans, sliced, or small whole ones, edible podded peas, green pepper strips, and broccoli flowerets.

Tempura Batter

½ cup flour
½ cup cornstarch
1 teaspoon salt
½ teaspoon monosodium glutamate
1½ teaspoon baking powder
1 egg
⅔ cup water

Sift together flour, cornstarch, salt, monosodium glutamate, and baking powder. Beat egg with water. Pour into dry ingredients and stir quickly. The batter should be lumpy. Prepare batter just before you plan to use it.

Tempura Dipping Sauce

3 cups *dashi* or chicken stock
2 tablespoons soy sauce
1 tablespoon sugar
½ teaspoon monosodium glutamate

Season *dashi* or chicken stock with soy sauce, sugar, and monosodium glutamate. Pour sauce into individual dipping bowls and have a small bowl of grated *daikon* to mix with the sauce.

Cooking tempura

I learned this technique from an old friend who was *tempura* chef at a restaurant. Use salad oil rather than a solid shortening for frying. Heat oil (enough to give an inch or two of sinking room) in a deep fat fryer or in a heavy kettle on the stove to 350°. An electric wok is particularly good for this. Dip each morsel in batter.

If it's shrimp, hold by the tail and dip one at a time. Use chopsticks, a slotted spoon, or your fingers to hold the vegetables. Dip in batter and drain the excess batter before putting in the hot oil. Drop gently into oil. They should sink to the bottom and immediately bob back up to the top. If they don't, the oil is too cold. If they brown too quickly, the oil is too hot.

Cook a few at a time until golden. Drain on paper towels.

After cooking, cool oil, then pour through a sieve into a bottle. Store in refrigerator. Combine this oil with fresh cooking oil the next time you prepare *tempura*. This combination of new and used oil helps to develop a deep brown color on the coating.

Shrimp with Chinese Peas

Snap off ends and pull side strings from 1 cup edible podded peas. Combine with ½ cup sliced water chestnuts, ½ cup sliced bamboo shoots, and 1 cup sliced fresh mushrooms. Follow basic recipe below.

Shrimp with Broccoli

Follow basic recipe using 1½ cups broccoli. Cut flowerets into bite-size pieces; cut stalks diagonally in pieces ½ inch long. Cut 1 onion in wedges and separate layers. Combine with ½ cup sliced bamboo shoots, and 4 dried mushrooms, pre-soaked and thinly sliced.

Shrimp with Eggplant

Roll-cut 1 Oriental eggplant and 1 zucchini. Cut 1 onion in wedges and separate layers. Cut 2 tomatoes in wedges. Follow basic recipe, cooking eggplant, zucchini, and onion 2 minutes. Add tomatoes and stir-fry 1 minute. Add 2 tablespoons water, cover, and cook 1 minute.

Basic Stir-Fried Shrimp

Salad oil for cooking
¼ teaspoon salt
½ pound uncooked shrimp, shelled and deveined
1 teaspoon minced ginger root
2 teaspoons *each* soy sauce and sherry
3 cups prepared vegetables (suggestions above)
½ teaspoon salt
2 tablespoons water (optional: depends on vegetables)

Gravy: 1 tablespoon cornstarch mixed with ½ cup chicken stock or water

1. Heat 2 tablespoons oil in wok or frying pan. Sprinkle with the ¼ teaspoon salt. Add shrimp and stir-fry for 1 minute. Add ginger and stir-fry for 1 minute. Add soy sauce and sherry and swish around pan for 1 minute. Remove from pan.

2. Heat 2 tablespoons oil in wok. Add vegetables; sprinkle with salt, and stir-fry for 2 minutes. If you are using vegetables that are very firm, add 2 tablespoons water and cover. Cook until vegetables are crisp tender, about 2 minutes. Return shrimp to pan. Stir gravy to recombine, pour into pan, and cook until thickened. Serves 4 to 5.

Oriental vegetable gardening

Your "Adventures in Oriental Cooking" are complete when the vegetables you use come from your own garden. Here the Chinese-American residents of Locke, California share with you their growing methods—the same as those used for years on the Pearl River Delta in China. And following, are additional vegetable varieties which you may want to add to your garden.

James Motlow, author and photographer of the following story, has been a resident of Locke, California since 1971. When he first arrived, Motlow lived on Main Street, and admits he was unaware of the intricate community which existed on Key Street, not quite a block away. Motlow moved to Key Street in 1973 and, because he was a newcomer, had difficulty being accepted. Today he is considered a member of the community. "My pictures aren't trophies of exotic people I've captured; they're my neighbors who are about me all the time," says Motlow. Currently Motlow is at work on a book dealing with the Chinese communities of the Sacramento River Delta; and a photography exhibit which will travel to the various Chinese communities in the state.

The town of Locke is located in the Sacramento Delta region of California. It began in 1912 with the construction of three buildings. It expanded during the years between 1915 and 1920 with more structures, most of which stand today. It remains today a unique Chinese community in America.

Locke was built as a separate community, not on the edges of an existing town as were most other Chinese settlements in this country. The town was founded by, and has always been inhabited by Chungshan Chinese. Chungshan refers to a district in Southern China where a dialect of Cantonese is spoken. The majority of Chungshan Chinese (a minority of the Chinese population in California) live in the Sacramento

◁

Since the early 1900's the vegetable gardens at Locke have provided residents with a major source of food.

Delta region. The Delta has much of the same climate and soil conditions as the Chungshan's native land, the Pearl River Delta in China.

Locke began by serving the needs of the local Chinese agricultural community. Six restaurants, five hotels and rooming houses, five grocery stores, one pool room, two cigar stands, a bakery, shoe repair store, theatre, lodge, post office, a Chinese school, and a church once made up Main Street, and part of the back streets of Locke. As the asparagus farming interests shifted further from Locke, the population of approximately five hundred began to dwindle. Many who had been raised in Locke later left for the nearby cities of

Sacramento, Stockton, San Francisco, and Los Angeles.

The town's present population is around seventy. Ninety percent are Chinese (all Chungshan), many of whom are first generation. The average age in town is 65 to 70; most are retired, living on fixed incomes. Unlike many others of the same age and economic situation, the people here describe their life with a single word: "satisfied."

The Locke gardens

Directly behind town are the gardens of Locke. Started originally as an area for "victory gardens," this half acre of land has provided a constant supply of vegetables for over thirty

Bok choy is hung out each morning during the drying period.

After many years of continual use and the yearly addition of organic matter, the soil in the gardens is easy to manage. Irrigation for established plants is accomplished by trenching for flooding between rows.

years. There exists here a balance between nature and people living in the twentieth century. Something is always going in the ground as something else is taken out.

The vegetables grown can be divided into two broad categories: cool-weather crops, and warm-weather crops.

All of the cool weather vegetables will survive the coldest winter days in Locke, but quickly bolt to seed when the weather warms.

These seasonal categories are not absolute. Some of the cool-weather vegetables can be planted in the garden while the weather is still quite warm, but for best results, predominately cool weather is required.

Basic good gardening practices and common sense are used throughout the garden. When plants are in the seed and seedling stage the watering is done with overhead sprinkling. As plants become established, trench irrigation is used. All planting is done in raised beds of well-worked soil. Rotation of vegetables from year to year is always practiced. Fertilizer consists of a combination of manure, compost, and ammonium sulphate. Insects are usually tolerated, and repellents used sparingly.

There are always enough vegetables for all; very little of anything is wasted. Plants not eaten are worked back into the soil or put into a compost. Many plants are dried and stored for later use. Seeds are saved from one year's harvest for next year's planting. Poles used for climbing vegetables are used time and time again. Even the string used to tie them together is saved and reused.

Gardening is of considerable importance, and is an integrated part of the daily life in Locke. The gardens provide a major source of food and a place for recreation. In summer, during the cool morning and evening hours, most of the town's population can be found in their gardens, exchanging talk and thoughts on vegetables and seeds.

Locke is listed in the National Register of Historical Places, and further historical information can be found in a Master Thesis, "Locke, California: Persistence and Change in the Cultural Landscape of a Delta Chinatown," 1975, by D. D. Arreola.

The warm-season crops

Cee Gwa or Cing Gwa—luffa or Chinese okra

This *gwa* is called *cee gwa,* except by gamblers, who have always referred to it as *sin gwa.* Simply, *cee* means lose and *sin* means win.

First planting should be in late spring when all danger of frost has passed and the ground is warm. Sow seeds 1 inch deep, 4 to 6 inches apart, in a raised bed of well-worked soil. There should be enough space between rows for easy walking and picking. Before plants are 3 inches high, make a frame 6 to 7 feet tall of poles stuck into the ground, one pole per plant, about 3 inches from the plant. Use crossbraces to complete the frame. The common practice is to tie the young vines loosely to the poles to get them on their way. Harvest time is about 60 days, lasting about 3 to 5 weeks.

Cee gwa is best for eating when

about 8 inches long, but size is no indication of freshness. Picking is very important because the plant will stop bearing if many *gwas* are left to mature on the vine. To get the full potential from *cee gwa,* pick early and frequently for eating, and allow a few to dry for scrubbers (luffas). For scrubbers, remove the dry skin by placing the fruit in a bucket of water for a few days (change the water daily) until the outer wall disintegrates. For cooking, peel and cut the young *gwa* into chunks and steam or stir-fry with pork or beef.

Doan Gwa—winter melon

Doan gwa should be started in late spring after the ground is thoroughly warm. There are two ways to grow this melon, but both are started in the same way. Plant two seeds 1 inch deep, 12 inches apart, in well-worked

A small Cee Gwa hangs from a bamboo trellis. Best for eating at about 8 inches.

Throughout the gardening season there's always something going into the garden while other vegetables are ready for harvest. Here, a basket of Gai Lohn *(broccoli)* was part of the morning harvest.

soil on the uppermost edge of a shallow trench. Make a bed of straw (in Locke the dried vines of spring snow peas are used) on the side of the trench where the vines will sprawl. The bed should be 2 inches thick, and 6 to 8 feet wide. Thin out the weaker plants, leaving one plant per foot. *Doan gwa* grows as a single-stalked vine. It is important that the mature plant be allowed to grow only on the bed. If allowed to spread too far, the damp ground can cause early fruit spoilage.

The other method of growing is the same, except that instead of laying a straw bed, the vines are trained to grow up and over an arbor. As the melon matures, it will need to be supported from the bottom. Old shirts work fine for *gwa* "slings".

Bigger is better for *doan gwas.* When mature, a white powder will appear on its surface. Remember that the position of the *gwa* when it was picked must be its position when stored. If stored otherwise, the water inside will shift and cause it to spoil. Store in a warm, dry place; a high shelf in the kitchen works fine.

Use *doan gwa* throughout the winter as a soup base. Peel it, then cut into quarters, eighths, or whatever happens to fit into a large pot. Save the seeds for next year's crop.

Dow Gauk—yardlong or asparagus bean

65 days from planting to harvest. Start after danger of frost is past, when ground is thoroughly warm. Plant 1 inch deep, 4 inches apart,

in well-worked soil, with side trenches for watering. Set out poles for the bean vines to climb. Use one pole per plant with cross braces between poles. (Bamboo poles, 6 to 7 feet tall work well for this purpose.) Remember that the vines will grow as high as the poles are tall. Because of the short harvest season, stagger plantings at three-week intervals to stretch the season. *Dow gauk* benefits greatly from fertilizing and frequent picking. The bean is stringless, so to prepare it you need only break into 2-inch sections and cook quickly, either stir-frying or steaming. For next year's planting, allow a few pods to dry on the vine so you'll have seed. Pick before the rains and tie together; store where they will be free from moisture.

Dow Gauk, *the asparagus or yardlong bean, requires a trellis to grow on. Frequent pickings necessary for good harvest.*

Bitter melons *are bitter, but a taste for them is quickly acquired.*

Foo Gwa—bitter melon

80 days until harvest. Sow seeds after all danger of frost has passed in thoroughly warm and well-worked soil. Plant 1 inch deep, 6 to 8 inches apart, with a watering trench alongside. This *gwa* is a climber and needs to hang in order to mature properly. Set out poles, one per plant, with cross braces between the poles. When 3 to 12 inches tall the young vine may need some help climbing. If so, tie loosely to the pole. When mature the fruit is 4 to 12 inches long, 2 inches in diameter, with ridges on its surface. Bitter melon is, as its name implies, bitter, but a taste for it is quickly acquired. The size of the plant is no indication of bitterness. The fruit's bitterness is determined by the length of time it is left to grow on the vine. The older the *gwa* is, the less cooking time is required. Accordingly, cook younger *gwa* for a longer period of time. *Foo gwa,* garlic, black beans, and pork combined make a unique-tasting Chinese dish.

To dry, thinly slice the *gwa,* set out in the open sun and allow to dry thoroughly. Store in a glass jar. To make one cup of *foo gwa* tea, combine three cups of water, a handful of dried bitter melon, one teaspoon black beans, and boil for thirty minutes.

For next year's crop, save the seeds from the biggest *foo gwa,* dry, and store in a jar.

Hin Choy

Plant seeds in spring; expect first harvest in 40 days. Harvest will continue until late summer. Scatter seeds in the same area as *yuen sai, chung fa,* and *gow choy* (see cool-season crops, page 86). Cover lightly with soil and water. After the first year *hin choy* will reseed itself, returning year after year. *Hin choy* has small, green, paddle-shaped leaves (other varieties have red leaves). They have a unique taste, unlike any Western green vegetable. The leaves have a light fuzz on them which is not objectionable to eat, and the *choy* is extremely tender after cooking. Use either steamed or in soups.

Mao Gwa— little winter melon

80 days until harvest. Grow in the same manner as *doan gwa* except this *gwa* must be allowed to climb and hang. When the vine is about ten inches tall, loosely tie to a pole (one pole per vine). Pick the *gwa* when it is small, (3 to 4 inches in diameter) and a light green. Peel, cut into chunks, and steam or stir-fry for eating; the taste is sweet and succulent. Save the seeds for next year's planting.

Poo Gwa— baseball-bat squash

Plant seeds in mounds of well-worked soil, after all chance of frost has passed and ground is thoroughly warm. Start with 3 to 5 seeds per mound, 1 inch deep, 2 inches apart. Thin later, allowing only the strongest seedling to remain. Space mounds 4 to 6 feet apart near a fence or some object on which vines can climb. An arbor is perhaps best, as it provides unobstructed hanging space for the *gwa.* When mature it should look like a baseball bat. Pick anytime after the squash has reached a length of 2 feet. The skin will remain tender even when it reaches 3 or more feet. One good *poo gwa* plant will produce more than enough for a family of four for about a month. It is a very easy vegetable to grow, highly recommended for the beginning home gardener.

Cook *poo gwa* like any other squash. It has a mild, subtle flavor, and goes well with almost any food.

For seed for next year's crop allow one or two squash to dry on the vine. Take indoors before the rains, and store in a place that is free from moisture. The dry *gwa* is very handsome and can be used decoratively.

The cool-season crops

Bok Choy

45 days until harvest. More *bok choy* is grown than any other vegetable in the Chinese winter garden. Plant in late summer and continue planting until spring. Scatter seeds ½ inch deep in a starter bed of well-worked soil and water. When 3 to 5 inches tall transplant young plants to shallow craters 2 inches deep. Space craters 10 to 14 inches apart in rows 15 to 18 inches apart in a raised bed. When mature, this *choy* is very tolerant of cold weather, but warm spring days

Mao Gwa, *the little winter melon, is sweet and succulent.*

Poo Gwa *are harvested after they reach two or three feet in length.*

Bok Choy *can take the cold, but bolts quickly in warm spring weather.*

The seasonal changes

As with any vegetable garden, the varieties planted in the Locke gardens vary by the season. Although the vegetables can be broken into two broad groups—cool-season and warm-season—they aren't mutually exclusive categories. As was pointed out, "something is always going into the ground as something else is taken out."

Because the available gardening space is limited (approximately 400 sq. ft.), Locke gardeners practice their own form of "intensive gardening," with each vegetable receiving almost individual attention. The garden plots are in continual use, so the rotation of crops is an essential part of the plan.

The warm-season crops include many varieties of squash and gourds. Because the gardening space is limited, training these vining vegetables on bamboo trellises is the best solution. Trellis training also allows full development of the fruit and keeps them off the moist soil, free from rot. The larger fruits require slings under them, tied to the trellis for support.

The cool-season crops include primarily the leafy vegetables, and vegetables that develop underground. Winters in Locke are comparatively mild, without snow, so the ground is workable throughout the cold season.

The only cool-season crop that requires a trellis is *ho lan do* (snow peas). Most cool-season crops are started in the early fall. Gardeners take advantage of the final warm days of fall, getting young plants off to a good start before the days shorten and the weather cools.

1 foot

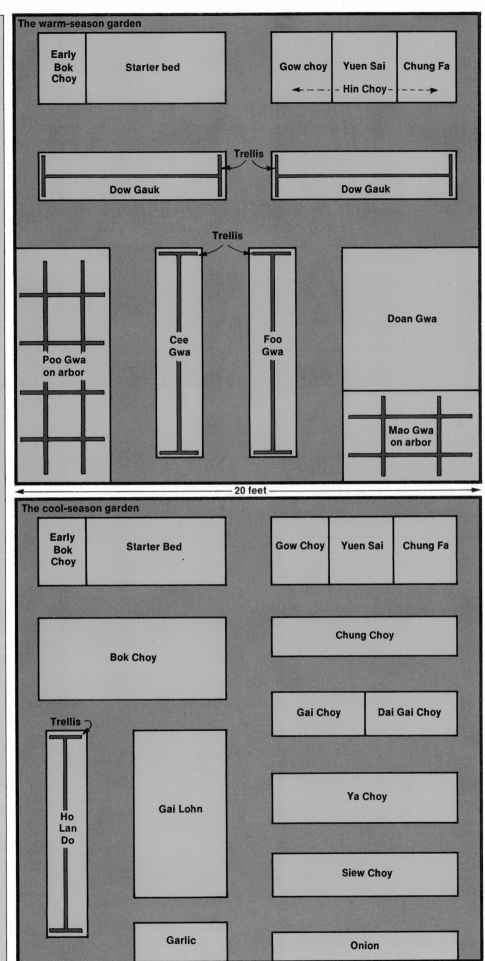

Left: An angled board protects early plantings of Ho Lan Do (snow peas) from cold north winds. Right: Later in the season a trellis is constructed from bamboo poles for the snow peas to climb on. Frequent pickings are a must.

will cause it to bolt. It has loose green leaves and a center stalk (heart), both of which are eaten. Like *gai lohn* many cuttings can be made from one plant. New leaves and a new heart will rapidly grow to replace cuttings you take. This vegetable is used in a variety of dishes, either stir-fried or steamed, and goes well with almost any combination of vegetables and meats.

In the spring much of the crop is dried for winter use. To dry, pull out the whole plant, and cut off the roots, leaving the leaves attached to the center (the heart may be cut out and eaten fresh). Wash, and boil the *bok choy* for 5 to 10 minutes and hang to dry on a clothes line. It will take three to five days to dry. Bring the *bok choy* in every night or cover it with plastic. When dry, wrap and store in a cool, dry place. Good for soups.

Allow one plant to go to seed. Pick and crack open the dried pods, remove the seeds and store in a jar for fall planting.

Chung Choy—turnip

Chung choy is not grown to be eaten fresh, but to be pickled. It is used as a flavoring agent in a variety of Chinese dishes. For a fall crop, plant in midsummer. Sow seeds ½ inch deep, ½ inch apart, in rows 8 inches apart in a bed of well-worked soil. Cover with some type of loose mulch (straw is very good) and water well. When the seedlings are 2 to 4 inches

tall remove the mulch and thin plants to 4 inches apart. Replant in late fall for an early spring crop, and again in late winter for a late spring crop.

To pickle, pull out the mature plants, wash, skin, and hang out to dry on a clothes line. After one to four days the plant will be about half dry, (this drying is mostly for shrinkage). Remove from the clothes line and rub salt into the *chung choy*. Alternate layers of *chung choy* and rock salt in a wide-mouthed container (a plastic bucket is fine), four to six layers high. Place a lid that fits *inside* the container, on top of the layers, and place a heavy object on it. Let stand for two weeks. Remove *chung choy* from the container, hang out to dry for two days, and then return to jar with lid tightly secured. Use in almost any dish for a special taste.

Chung Fa—green onions

Sometimes referred to as multiplying, or green onions. *Chung fa* can be planted anytime of the year, but will bolt much sooner in the summer. Start seeds by scattering over an area of well-worked soil, and water often. An established clump can be taken out, separated, and put back into the ground. One clump will keep reproducing until summer. Bolting can be retarded by planting *chung fa* in a shaded area. For fall planting, allow a clump to go to seed. Dry and separate the seeds and store. *Chung fa* is usually planted in the same

area with *gow choy* (chives), and *yuen sai* (parsley). Use this onion fresh as a final ingredient to all types of vegetable and meat dishes.

Dai Gai Choy—mustard

65 days from planting to harvest. Start seeds ½ inch deep in a starter bed of well-worked soil. During cold-winter months, start seeds indoors in cut-off milk cartons. When 3 to 5 inches tall, transplant outdoors into shallow craters 2 inches deep. Space craters 10 to 15 inches apart in rows 15 to 18 inches apart. Except during the coldest winter months, the seeds can be started outdoors. The mature plant is very hardy and is not affected by low temperatures. The last harvest should be planned for early spring; warmer days will cause bolting.

Dai gai choy has large green leaves and a broad stem. The taste is similar to that of *gai choy* except that it has a sharper flavor. It is best served with fish or pork dishes.

Gai Choy—mustard

35 days until harvest. Plant in fall, like *gai lohn,* in a scattered fashion, and covering with a thin layer of soil. When seedlings are 3 to 5 inches tall, transplant to a raised bed. Plant transplants in small craters 2 inches deep, 10 to 12 inches apart, in rows 15 to 18 inches apart. During the winter start seedlings indoors. Transplant outdoors when days become warm. Mature plants are very hardy

and can withstand the coldest winter days. Young plants are tender, so take steps to protect them from frost. Plant in late summer for a winter harvest and in late winter for a spring harvest. *Gai choy* is very easy to grow. Its leaves and stems are light green. The taste is mild, clear, and not pungent. Delicious in soups, or stir-fried with other vegetables and meat.

Gai Lohn—broccoli

70 days until harvest. Sow seeds in late summer, scattering them over a small area. Cover with a thin (¼-inch) layer of well-worked soil, and water. Transplant when 3 to 5 inches tall into shallow holes 6 to 10 inches apart. Space rows 12 to 15 inches apart on a raised bed of well-worked soil. This method of dense planting helps in weed control and gives easy access to a steady supply of *gai lohn*. Use side trenches and overhead sprinkling to water.

Gai lohn is usually compared to the common broccoli, but there is only a slight similarity in taste. Its leaves are used as well as the stalk (the heart), which grows from the plant's center. Keeps bearing after repeated cuttings. The heart and leaves are best when young. When the heart is old, peel before cooking to expose the more tender and flavorable meat. Stir-fry *gai lohn* and *bok choy* together with some meat and a little bit of ginger.

The *gai lohn* harvest ends in midspring when warm days cause it to bolt. Allow a few plants to bolt and go to seed. When dry, remove pods from the plant and crack to free the seeds inside. Store seeds free from moisture. Any plants that are not used for eating or for seeds can be pulled up, cut into pieces, and worked into the soil, or put into a compost pile.

Gow Choy—chives

Scatter seeds ½ inch deep in well-worked soil. *Gow choy, chung fa,* and *yuen sai* are generally planted in the same space. All will reappear in the fall if left to reseed themselves. To harvest, cut off near the base. Cut in 1 to 1½ inch lengths. Add to stir-fried dishes or eggs or use in soup.

Ho Lan Do— sugar or snow pea

Seeds should be planted in late fall for spring harvest. Make only two plantings, two to three weeks apart. Plant seeds 1 inch deep, 6 inches apart, in a 2-foot-wide raised bed of well-worked soil. Plants should be about 2 feet tall before cold winter weather sets in. Build a frame for the peas to climb (bamboo poles are good for this purpose), using one pole per plant. If your poles are too long the peas will grow too high for easy picking. Birds love young sprouting snow peas, so protect them until they are about 3 to 5 inches high. Set out flags and some type of noise maker (colorful rags and pie tins are great) to keep birds away. When tall enough tie plants to poles for a good start. When winter arrives the plants will go dormant and stop growing; this is normal, don't pull them out. When the weather begins to warm, the waking *ho lan do* will shoot up and grow to the height of the frame and begin to bear. *Ho lan do* benefits from frequent picking. Figure on about three weeks of good harvests. You can eat the whole tender pea pods, raw or cooked, in a variety of dishes. For next year's seeds, pick a dozen or so large pods, tie them together and hang out to dry. Store pods where they will be free from moisture. In late fall break open the pods and plant the seeds.

Siew Choy & Ya Choy— cabbage

80 days till harvest. Start seeds in late summer ½ inch deep in a starter bed of well-worked soil. Transplant when 3 to 5 inches tall in shallow craters, 1 to 3 inches deep. Space craters 12 inches apart, in rows 18 inches apart on a raised bed. These *choys* can be planted through the fall until the ground becomes too cold for good germination. Mature plants are not harmed by cold weather, but will quickly bolt when the weather turns warm. As the heads grow larger, the leaves will need to be tied together loosely. The head is closed and tapered with pale green leaves. The one difference between these two *choys* is that *siew choy* is slightly sweeter than *ya choy*. These are versatile vegetables and can be eaten raw in a salad, or cooked in many stir-fried dishes.

Yuen Sai—Chinese parsley

50 days till harvest. Best grown as a cool-season crop, but *yuen sai* can also be grown in summer if planted only once every few years; it reseeds itself freely. To plant, crack the seeds, being careful not to smash them. Scatter into a well-worked soil about ¼ inch deep, and water often. *Yuen sai* is also known as Chinese parsley. It looks like parsley except the leaves are flatter, a lighter shade of green, and more feathery. The fragrance is aromatic and very distinct. The fresh leaves and stems can be sprinkled over most meat, poultry, and seafood dishes.

Freshly-cut grass protects tender seedlings from frost early in the season.

Gow Choy (chives) will reseed itself in fall if flowers are left on the plant.

More about Oriental vegetables

It's difficult, at least at first, to plan and plant a garden with Oriental cooking in mind. It's not that the vegetables are difficult to grow, but the fact that each variety goes by a multitude of names. Behind each name is another name in another language, and behind that name another in a local dialect. The photograph at left will help identify many of the vegetables which are known by a variety of names.

When checking for seed sources for these vegetables, check your standard seed catalogs first. Many of the vegetables which are labeled Oriental have been around a long time in regular seed catalogs, and have been planted because of their good taste, special climate adaptability, or the need of harvest variety from the garden.

On page 96 we have assembled a list of seed catalogs and their addresses that specialize in Oriental vegetables, and others that specialize in unusual items, including many Oriental varieties.

Arrowhead

Arrowhead is a swamp plant grown for its edible corms. It is a common, popular water garden plant in the U.S. The plant gets its name from the shape of its leaves, not the shape of the corm.

Depending on the fertility of the soil, arrowhead plants will rapidly develop eight or more corms per plant. The corms are usually harvested in fall.

Gobo—burdock

Throughout the mainland states, burdock is a weed; in Hawaii it's grown commercially for its edible root. You may know burdock for its long

A collection of both Japanese and Chinese vegetables: 1. Oriental cucumber, 2. Soy bean sprouts, 3. Mung bean sprouts, 4. canned bamboo sprouts, 5. Yardlong beans, 6. Luffa gourd, 7. Fuzzy melon, 8. Bitter melon, 9. Chayote, 10. Japanese pickling melon, 11. Fresh soybeans, 12. Baseball bat squash, 13. Calabash, 14. Japanese pumpkins (two varieties), 15. Water chestnuts, 16. Edible podded snow peas, 17. Arrowhead, 18. Chinese parsley, 19. Shiso, 20. Chinese mustard greens, 21. Burdock (gobo), 22. Daikon, 23. Oriental eggplant, 24. Yama imo, 25. Ginger root, 26. Chinese chives, 27. Winter melon, 28. Chinese cabbage, 29. Chinese broccoli, 30. Kohlrabi, 31. Hearts of Bok Choy, 32. Bok Choy, 33. Broadleaf mustard, 34. Broadleaf mustard (often sold this way—without leaves on top).

stalks, broad leaves, and large, sharp burrs. Its burrs have earned it common names like "beggar's button," and "clothbur." The Japanese call it gobo.

Gobo (burdock) has little food value, but contains fair amounts of carbohydrates. The root is used as an ingredient in many Oriental dishes. Its texture is rather chewy even when cooked. Gobo has no flavor of its own. The flavor of gobo is the flavor of what it is cooked with.

Gobo is grown the same way as carrots, requiring a deep, loose soil for root development.

Fuki—Butterbur

Butterbur is used in both Japanese and Chinese cooking. You'll see it in specialty stores under the name "coltsfoot" as well. The Japanese name for it is fuki. It grows as a large perennial, in moist, rich soil. It has large, roundish leaves, supported by heavy stems, which are the edible portion of the plant. Butterbur is most frequently seen as an imported canned product from Japan.

Calabash gourd

Calabash is a name applied to gourds of many shapes. The important thing to remember when growing gourds is that they are a warm-season crop, requiring a long season to produce a full crop of gourds.

Seeds can be planted directly in fertile soil, or started indoors where short-growing seasons are a problem. Plant at the edge of the garden, or on a trellis—they'll spread 20 feet or more.

Young immature gourds can be eaten; they are usually steamed until just tender. Mature gourds, from 3 to 6 feet long, are dried and used for a variety of utilitarian purposes.

Chayote

This member of the gourd family is native to Mexico and Central America. It is becoming increasingly available in American specialty produce markets. Pronounced chy-OH-tee, this pear-shaped gourd is also known by the name vegetable pear, custard marrow, one-seeded cucumber and to the Creoles, merliton.

The plant is a perennial vine that is evergreen in tropical climates. In mild winter areas, frost kills the tops each winter, but the vine renews itself each spring. Very fast growing, it will cover a 10- to 15-foot section of fence with large, lobed leaves by midsummer.

The whole fruit is used as "seed." Plant it with the large end sloping downward into the soil, and with the small end slightly exposed.

In cold-winter climates, add a deep winter mulch—10 inches or more of compost, which you pull aside at sprouting time when the weather warms in spring.

Give the plants the same treatment as a strong-growing gourd: Plenty of organic matter—manure or compost in the planting hole—generous feeding and watering when the plant growth is under way. Go easy on the water at the start; overwatering will rot the seed.

Store chayote fruits in a cool (no less than 50°) place. They will keep

Arrowhead corms. Its name comes from the shape of the leaves.

for two or three months for later eating, or for use in seeding in the spring. If they send out shoots in storage, which is likely, cut the shoots back to 2 inches when you plant.

Chayote can be cooked without peeling, if the peel is tender. If not, wash it, peel, and then dice or slice. Cut completely through the flat inner seed; it is edible and has a nutlike flavor after cooking. It can be used in as many ways as squash—and more.

Chinese or celery cabbage

The forms of Chinese cabbage receive a variety of names in the seed catalogs, and since it will be from the catalogs that you will choose them, we let the catalogs describe the varieties. There are two heading types of Chinese cabbage: the tall one and the squat one. The difference is in manner of growth only. The change in the catalogs in the last year or two has been the introduction of the *wong bok* type called, in one form or another, hybrid Chinese cabbage.

This is a description of *wong bok* and hybrid Chinese cabbage:

"A great hybrid Chinese cabbage for home gardeners. Its earliness, husky growth, and fine quality have made it popular, and best of all, it does not bolt quickly to seed in early plantings like other Chinese cabbage—it may be grown as an early spring crop as well as in the fall. Ready about ten days earlier than *michihili*, it has a shorter, broader shape. Its crumpled leaves fold well over the tops. Once you've tried it,

you're sure to delight in the spicy flavor of Chinese cabbage."

This is the description of *michihili*: "The finest strain of this popular type. A long-standing favorite with gardeners. A uniform, dependable strain, it heads evenly and remains in prime condition for a long time. When mature the firm, long heads are 18 inches tall and 3½ to 4 inches thick, slightly tapered at the top. Blanching pure white inside, they are tender, crisp, and sweet with an agreeably spicy flavor."

Chinese cabbage is found year around in supermarkets, but there is a distinct difference between spring and fall crops. Cabbages harvested in late spring and early summer tend toward coarse green leaves and a head that is not well formed. This is because cabbages are low-sunlight crops, and in the spring, when sunlight is longer during the day, cabbages tend to flower quickly. Spring and summer cabbage is generally used for stir-frying, or in other cooked dishes. Crops harvested in late fall and winter are fully headed with more blanched leaves, which are generally milder and more tender, and excellent in salads.

Thus, the most favorable months for planting are July, August, and September, depending on the expected date of the first frost.

Plant seeds ½ inch deep, 8 to 16 seeds per foot. Seedlings transplant easily. They can be thinned gradually, with fully grown cabbage needing 10

to 14 inches of space. The home gardener can conserve space by thinning gradually, a few inches at a time. When plants to be thinned are 8 to 10 inches tall, they can be harvested and prepared similar to mature cabbage. Chinese cabbage takes 70 to 75 days to fully mature.

Chinese green mustard cabbage

This mustard cabbage (also sold as India mustard) has a wider spread than the Chinese white mustard cabbage and should be spaced 15 inches apart in the row. However, plants are often set at closer intervals in early spring to be harvested at the 5- to 6-leaf stage. Mustard cabbage is often eaten raw with a hot sauce of chili pepper and soy sauce. There are many cultivated varieties of the Oriental mustards. Leaf size, color, and flavor vary. Each locality has its favorite.

Bok Choy—Chinese mustard cabbage

Other names for this cabbage include Chinese white mustard cabbage, *pak choy* or *pok choi,* and spoon cabbage. It is a nonheading type of Chinese cabbage that resembles Swiss chard, with heavy white stalks. It is a popular ingredient in mixed vegetable dishes served in Chinese restaurants and is valued for the compact, blanched heart sometimes sold in specialty markets.

A cool-season crop, it should be planted at the same time as the heading type of Chinese cabbage.

Chayote is produced on a fast growing vine. Fruit weighs up to one pound.

Like many Oriental vegetables, Chinese cabbage (in wooden box) adapt well to container growing.

In fall, *bok choy* matures more quickly than Chinese cabbage, usually in 65 days. It also requires less room between the plants in the row—between 6 to 8 inches. Winter and spring crops should be harvested when flower buds first appear.

Oriental cucumber

There are many varieties of Oriental cucumber, and common to them all is their extra-long size and mild flavor.

Where the growing season is short, start seed indoors 4 to 6 weeks before time to set out transplants. When setting out transplants, cover plants with "hot caps" or plastic to increase temperatures and protect from frost early in the season.

Cucumbers respond to generous amounts of organic matter in the soil. For special treatment, dig the planting furrow 2 feet deep and fill the first foot or so with manure mixed with peat moss, compost, sawdust, or other organic material. Fill rest of the furrow with soil, peat moss, and 5-10-10 fertilizer at the rate of 2 pounds to 50 feet of row.

Since roots will grow to a depth of 3 feet if soil is normal, watering should be slow and deep. If the plant is under stress from lack of moisture at any time, it just stops growing. It will pick up again when moisture is supplied. It is normal for leaves of cucumbers to wilt in the middle of the day during hot spells, but check the soil for moisture at the below-surface levels.

Cucumbers trained on a trellis take very little ground space and you will harvest more attractive, straighter fruits, and have fewer culls.

Don't worry about the failure of the first early flowers to set fruit. The male flowers open first, then about a week later you'll see flowers with baby cucumbers at their bases. The male flowers supply the pollen which is transferred by insects to the female flowers.

Keep all fruit picked from the vines as they reach usable size. The importance of this can't be overstressed, because even one fruit left to mature on the plant will completely stop the set of new fruit.

The correct way to pick a cucumber is to turn the fruit parallel to the vine and snap it sharply. In this way its stem breaks off cleanly and the vine is not damaged.

Daikon—Oriental radish

Oriental radishes are white with large roots measuring 12 to 18 inches long. Deep soil preparation is an obvious necessity. They can be grown through-

The long roots of daikon *(Oriental radish) require loose, friable soil.*

out the year in mild-winter coastal areas of California but are best planted in late summer or early spring.

Seed catalogs list many "fall and winter" radishes as well as the *daikon*. Several are offered for their giant size.

Oriental radishes are usually pickled and sold in the market as *takuan*. They can be grated and used as a condiment. For a cocktail snack, thinly slice *daikon* and marinate in *namasu* dressing. See page 40.

Dasheen

This is a cultivated variety of the well-known *taro* of Hawaii from which *poi* is made, and appears under the name of dasheen in the markets around the New Year holidays.

It's a fast-growing perennial, evergreen only in frost-free areas. It makes a handsome tub plant with giant elephant-ear leaves, 2 feet long and a foot wide, carried on 4- to 5-foot stalks.

Small corms are used as "seed" and planted as soon as the ground is warm. The tubers are harvested in late fall. As the tubers divide during

the growing season, they tend to grow on the surface. Compost added as a mulch to keep the corms covered and the ground moist produces excellent growth.

Dasheen reportedly contains less calcium oxalate than *taro*. However, the tubers are usually boiled first to destroy calcium oxalate crystals and then used in mixed vegetables and meat dishes or fried in strips or slices for chips.

Oriental eggplant

Oriental eggplant varieties are smaller and narrower than most of the eggplants you see in the supermarket, and require less summer heat for maturing.

Don't rush the season with eggplant. Set out plants only after the weather has consistently warmed up—when daytime temperatures are in the 70° range. You'll get a higher-quality fruit when development is rapid and uninterrupted by cool weather.

Eggplant makes an attractive container plant, and does very well in a 5-gallon can or box. Place the container in one of the warmer spots in your garden for best results.

Oriental eggplant varieties produce long, slender fruits.

The knobby roots of ginger can be planted outdoors in warm weather.

Eggplant should be used just after harvest as a *fresh* vegetable, not held in storage. For best eating quality, eggplant should be harvested when the fruit slows in growth and the skin is dark and glossy. If not harvested at this time, the mature fruit will lose its gloss, and will not be as tender when cooked.

Harvest the fruits regularly as they reach a usable size; oval varieties when 4 to 6 inches long, and 3 to 4 inches wide; long, slim types, 5 to 6 inches long, and 2 to 3 inches in diameter. When fruits are harvested at the immature stage, plants will usually set more fruits than if one or two fruits are allowed to reach full maturity.

Fuzzy melon

Fuzzy melon is a warm-season crop, usually seeded in midspring and harvested in summer. It should be planted where it has plenty of room to grow, or trained on a trellis.

Fuzzy melons are harvested soon after the flowers drop off, while the fruit is still quite immature. The shape of the fruit is usually square or oblong, but can be cylindrical, measuring up to 6 inches in diameter. Fuzzy melon is used in soups, stir-fried, or stuffed with meat and steamed.

Ginger

The spice we know as ginger comes from a plant belonging to the *Zingiberaceae* family. These include many attractive ornamentals that grow wild in tropical climates. Ginger is obtained from the bulbous root or rhizome of one of these ornamentals, *Zingiber officinale*. Grown for many centuries in India, ginger root is now commercially cultivated in Hawaii, Jamaica, and other tropical island groups.

The plant grows to a height of 3 feet with narrow leaves up to a foot long and about 1 inch wide. Yellowish-green flowers with yellow-spotted lips appear in dense cone-shaped spikes 3 inches long.

Ginger can be grown in this country in the summer months, or potted as an indoor or greenhouse plant. Obtain some of the knobby root from a market that specializes in Oriental foods or herbs and spices. Plant it, with the sprout end up, in rich, moist soil in a pot or in the ground if you live where days are hot and sunny. Be sure it has good drainage, lots of sun, and is in a spot that is protected from low temperatures and high winds.

The ginger plant has a unique back-to-front growing habit, and after the plant has matured, it will grow new sprouts out of the ground in front of it. Dig up one of these young sprouts and you will find a tender, new growth of bulbous root, subtler and fresher in seasoning quality than the older, sharper-tasting roots bought in the market.

The new sprouts themselves, cut when just a few inches tall (the root will sprout again), are also edible, and much sought after by Chinese and Japanese cooks.

To use ginger root, simply cut off what you need, peel, and finely chop or grate it. The young, slender greens of the ginger plant are delicious after marinating in vinegar, oil and a small amount of sugar.

Store ginger root in the refrigerator, or freezer, wrapped in plastic film or sealed in a plastic bag.

Lotus

The lotus plant *(Nelumbo* of the waterlily family) has been admired since prehistoric times for its showy, waterborne blossoms. Surprisingly, it is not only ornamental, but also edible, in all of its parts; the people of the Orient and East India have been eating its tuberous roots, leaves, flowers, and seeds for centuries.

Two varieties of lotus are commonly grown: the American lotus *(Nelumbo pentapetala)* and the East Indian *(N. nucifera)*. The American lotus is native to the eastern (as far north as New Jersey) and southeastern regions of our country. It has showy, fragrant blooms and large (1 to 2 feet across) blue-green leaves that stand 2 feet above the water.

If you have a good-sized garden pool and if you would like to try it, plant seed in pots and add a top layer of clean sand to the soil to keep the water clean. Submerge in 6 to 8 inches of water. Set 6 inches deeper when the plants begin to grow.

The distinctive lotus root occupies an important place in Chinese and Japanese cuisines. It is a commercial crop in Hawaii, where it is raised for shipment to the Orient and the mainland. It resembles a string of sausages in its linklike shape. Slice and use it in Oriental stir-fried dishes, or cut the leaves when young and boil as you would other greens. Pick the flowers and use the petals in clear soups and green salads.

Lotus seed pods can be dried and are popular in dried flower arrangements because of their unusual shape.

Mung beans

The mung bean is grown primarily for its tender and flavorful sprouts. In the garden it is treated as any other pole bean. It produces yellow flowers followed by 3-inch curving pods. Each of these contains a dozen or more small, round beans.

Mung beans make a tasty dish when boiled until tender, puréed in a blender and seasoned with soy sauce. This bean purée makes a delicious dip or spread.

To produce the sprouts, place one cup of bean seeds in a gallon glass jar. Secure a double thickness of cheesecloth over the opening with a strong rubber band. Fill the jar half full with water and let sit overnight. The next day drain off this water by inverting the jar (still secured with cheesecloth) and slightly tilting it to one side. This will allow drainage of the water and circulation of fresh air around the seeds. Place the jar in a slightly warm, dark location, such as a cupboard.

Rinse the seeds with water and drain, in the above manner, twice a day, always replacing the jar in a dark place. Continue until tiny sprouts appear (after 4 or 5 days).

When the first set of true leaves appears, the sprouts are ready to use. Don't remove the root fibers or loose hulls from the sprouts—much of the flavor and vitamins are contained in these.

The unwashed bean sprouts should be stored in a plastic bag in the refrigerator, to be used as soon as possible.

Bean sprouts make a fine addition to a tossed green salad, and are an essential ingredient when making chop suey, chow mein, and fried egg rolls. They also make a tasty side dish when stir-fried with thin slices of green onion and flavored with soy sauce.

Chinese parsley

If you see the leaves of this ancient herb *(Coriandrum sativum)* in the market, they'll be labeled Chinese parsley, cilantro, or coriander, and look something like parsley. The pungent flavor of the leaves is important in Chinese cooking and the aromatic quality of the seeds makes them useful in potpourris, confections, and many delicious dishes.

The plant is a fast-growing annual that reaches a height of about 1 to 2½ feet. It has oval leaves with serrated edges on the main stems and feathery, more delicate leaves on the side branches. The small flowers grow in parasol-shaped clusters and are pinkish-white in color. The plant gives off a kind of crushed-bug odor some people find offensive.

Coriander is an easy plant to grow. It likes sun or filtered shade, and light, well-drained soil. Sow the seeds in place in early spring and thin the plants 7 to 10 inches apart.

If you'd like a continuous and convenient supply of only the leaves, plant Chinese parsley in containers indoors or out, and harvest the leaves when they reach 6 inches in height. Sow new seeds every two weeks to insure a continuous supply.

For plants sown in the garden, pick the leaves sparingly, beginning when the plants are 4 to 6 inches tall. They will provide you with a good supply for a few months. In midsummer, gather the seeds as they ripen, or their weight will bend the stems and they'll fall off.

Place the stems in a jar or other container of water; slip a plastic bag over the leaves and refrigerate. In Oriental cooking, the fresh leaves are often used for a garnish. The leaves can also be chopped and frozen, or dried whole or ground, like other leafy herbs.

Mitsuba—Japanese parsley

Japanese parsley is a perennial which grows like watercress— in damp, shady locations. Seed can be sown directly in the garden in spring, or in a flat filled with a light soil mix. Be sure to keep it damp and cool.

Japanese parsley should be used when young and tender; older leaves tend to be tough. The leaves and stalks can be used in soups as a flavoring and a garnish. The plant will reseed itself if allowed to flower.

Japanese pickling melon

Japanese pickling melons are produced on very dense vines that spread 10 feet or more. They can be grown on the ground.

The Japanese pickling melon is another warm-season crop, treated in much the same way as melons and gourds. The melons are harvested

There are many cultivated varieties of mustard cabbage; each locality has its favorites. It's a cool-season crop.

The tuberous root of the showy water plant, lotus, sliced in thin rounds.

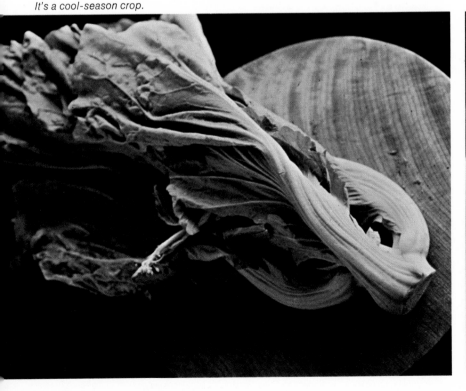

The many unusual shapes and forms of Japanese pumpkins make them ornamental as well as edible. A warm-season crop.

The young and tender leaves of shiso are used as a pungent garnish.

when they are almost full-grown, turning a greenish-white color. The harvest season usually lasts 4 to 6 weeks.

Japanese pumpkin

The Japanese pumpkin is a warm-season crop, produced on a large vine which spreads from 15 to 20 feet. The fruit is left on the vine until it turns color, and is then harvested and can be stored through the winter.

Like the winter melon, the unharvested fruit of the Japanese pumpkin should be kept dry, away from soil moisture.

Shiso

Shiso is an annual plant, the seeds of which should be sown in a sunny location in late spring. Seeds need a period of dormancy in order to germinate. Use either last year's seeds for this year's planting, or put new seeds in the refrigerator for a week and then plant. Seeds which have not gone through this dormancy period will take up to 30 days to germinate.

There are several varieties, but the purple is most commonly used. The young, tender leaves are used as a garnish, valued for their pungent flavor.

Shogoin—Japanese turnip

Seed catalogs may call this the foliage turnip. It's described as: "Quick-growing, 30 days to use foliage, 70 days for roots. Tops are 18 to 20 inches tall, plentiful, tender and mild.

When mature it produces roots that are 3 to 4 inches thick, flattened globe-shaped, with white skin and delicious tasting, fine-grained flesh."

Turnips do well in both spring and fall planting, maturing in 60 days, or less. The short season of the turnip permits it to be grown, at some time, everywhere in the U.S.

General soil and nutrient requirements are about the same as for beets. The seed bed need not be extremely fine because seedlings come quickly and easily and the enlarged roots are borne partly out of the ground.

Thin in stages to 1 to 2 inches apart, using the last thinnings for greens. Keep the crop well watered and growing fast for best quality.

Shungiku—garland chrysanthemum

Shungiku is often referred to as chop suey greens in the markets and on seed packets. *Shungiku* can be grown as a perennial and the removal of the edible, leafy shoots will not destroy the plant. The luxuriant young growth is usually harvested during the cooler parts of the year. The young shoots are coarse, stringy, and not very palatable during the summer months.

After checking reference books *Hortus* and Bailey's *Manual of Cultivated Plants,* it appears that there are two species of garland chrysanthemum. The species *Chrysanthemum coronarium* is native to the

Mediterranean, growing 3 to 4 feet tall with white or yellowish flowers. The species *C. spatiosum* is native to China, growing 2 feet or more with yellow flowers and leaves larger and more succulent than those of *C. coronarium.*

The description of chop suey greens or *shungiku* in the Park's seed catalog reads: "Aromatic greens cooked and grown like spinach. Harvest when plants are 4 to 5 inches tall. Sow early, 2 feet apart in rows, covering ½ inch with fine soil. Aromatic flavor. Easy culture."

The words "aromatic flavor" mean that the cooked leaves taste very much like the smell of chrysanthemum flowers and foliage.

These directions fit the Chinese species; the plant has the ability to grow from seed to 4 or 5 inches tall in a short growing season.

Uncooked they're considered too overwhelming in flavor for most tastes. Cut leaves into 2-inch lengths, and boil or stir-fry them to be served by themselves or in mixed-vegetable dishes.

Soybeans

Soybeans *(Glycine max* of the legume family) were cultivated in China in 3000 B.C., and since earliest times have been an all-important food (second only to rice) in Manchuria, Korea and Japan. They were first brought to the United States in 1804 but were used mainly as a forage crop until

1920. The big boom in commercial planting for seed began in 1942 as a result of the wartime demand for edible oils and fats.

Soybeans are now being recognized as a superior and most nutritious home-garden vegetable. As a fresh vegetable the beans are picked in the immature or green-shelled stage.

One characteristic of the soybean plant that sets it apart from all other beans is its time clock. It gets its signal for flowering from the sky. Short nights (long days) delay flowering; long nights (short days) speed up flowering.

Soybeans are as easy to grow as snap bush beans and are treated in the same way.

Avoid cultivating or working around beans when they are wet from rain, as the plants are easily bruised and broken.

They need inoculation with a commercial culture of nitrogen-fixing bacteria, unless the bacteria are known to be in the soil. Use an inoculant specifically prepared for soybeans; those containing bacteria from other legumes are not effective on soybeans. Follow the directions on the container.

The beans are ready to use as soon as the pods are plump and seeds are nearly full size but still green. All of the beans on the plant ripen about the same time, so you might as well pull the plant and find a shady spot to pick the pods.

Soybeans are not shelled like peas or lima beans. The best method of shelling is to pour boiling water over the pods and leave them in the hot water for 5 minutes, and then drain and cool. After this treatment it is easy to break the pods crosswise and squeeze out the beans.

Serve the beans cool, still in the pod. This is commonly done in Japan and adds to the enjoyment of eating, especially among the younger set.

Spinach

When Oriental vegetables are considered as a group, the spinach substitutes are included. They have been around a long time as standard seed catalog items.

Generally included with the malabar and tampala spinach varieties is the summer-tolerant New Zealand spinach, a low-growing ground cover-type plant. The young, tender stems and leaves can be cut repeatedly through the summer. Seeds for New Zealand spinach are widely available.

Malabar spinach. An attractive, glossy-leaved vine that grows rapidly when weather warms, to produce edible leaves in 70 days. Train it against a fence or wall. Young leaves and growing tips can be cut throughout the summer. A customer of the Burpee Seed Co. writes: "I have grown malabar spinach for several years. It is indeed not only a good vegetable but an ornamental plant. I prefer sprigs of this in water in the house for winter greenery to any ivy; in spring I cut the

The nutritious and easy to grow soybean.

sprigs into pieces and each joint will root in my propagating box and when danger of frost is over they go into my garden, not the vegetable garden but on ornamental frames for their beauty and picking the leaves to cook."

Malabar spinach may be used as cooked greens, or fresh in a salad.

Different types of "greens" appear at different times of the year in Japanese markets. Each has its own characteristic texture and flavor. Top left: squash greens. Bottom left to right: sweet potato greens, taro stems and leaves, and bitter melon greens.

Tampala. This tropical is a close relative of the amaranthus of the flower garden. In the opinion of those who grow it, it is sweeter and more tasty than spinach. Tender young leaves need only a few minutes to cook.

Water chestnut

The Chinese water chestnut (*Eleocharis dulcis,* of the sedge family) has been cultivated in the Orient and other parts of Asia for centuries. A kind of aquatic rush plant, it is grown in rice paddies under the names *ma-tai* in China and *kuro-kuwai* in Japan.

Water chestnuts are best grown in containers filled halfway with ordinary topsoil. Mix into this a tablespoon of granular, slow-release fertilizer. Fill the pot the rest of the way and plant the corm ¼ inch below the surface of the soil. Submerge the pot in a container of water or a shallow pool so that its soil surface is ½ to 2 inches below the surface of the water.

When the foliage dies down, tap the entire plant out of the pot. With a hose, wash the soil from the root mass, and gather the small brown chestnuts.

Placed back in soil underwater, water chestnuts will keep for a long time. Corms are available from Van Ness Water Gardens, 2460 N. Euclid Crescent West, Upland, CA 91786.

Sansho

The fresh leaves of sansho (also known as 'Japanese pepper leaf') are used as a pungent garnish, primarily in soups. The leaves are also dried and sold in a powdered form as a pepper substitute. Sansho grows as a small, shrubby tree, the seeds for which are difficult to obtain. The most frequent method of propagation is from slips of existing plants.

Chinese winter melon

This vegetable is grown in the same way as winter squash and pumpkins, and covers as much ground as the most vigorous pumpkins. The fruits

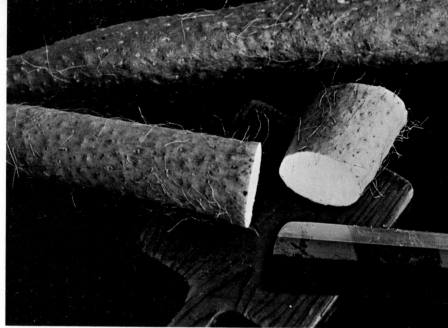

The slender tubers of the Japanese yam can reach 3 feet in length. They are left in the ground for 3 to 4 years to develop to this size.

will reach 20 to 40 pounds when mature. Maturing fruits may rot if soil is constantly moist under the melons.

Mature Chinese winter melons can be filled with chicken broth and steamed for several hours for soup, or cooked as a vegetable. Be sure melon is mature before cooking. This is indicated by a waxy coating on the surface. The melon is also used in combination with lotus rhizomes, kumquats, ginger, and sugar to make sweet preserves. (See also, *Doan Gwa,* page 82.)

Yama Imo—Japanese yam

If you know that the moist-fleshed sweet potato usually called a yam is not a yam but *Ipomoea batatas,* we can compare the Japanese yam to the sweet potato with a better understanding. The tubers of the Japanese yam are long and slender, 24 to 36 inches long as compared to the 6- to 10-inch sweet potato. Above ground the vines spread to 6 feet or more, twice the space needed for sweet potatoes.

Japanese yams are grown commercially in Hawaii and California. These yams, unlike sweet potatoes, are left in the ground for three to four years, in which time they become increasingly larger. The upper 4- to 6-inch portion of the tubers are replanted as seed pieces.

The white flesh of the fresh yams is grated or shredded, quickly turns mucilaginous and is served with soy sauce as a delicacy. The yam is a staple in Japanese cookery.

Seed sources

W. Atlee Burpee Co.
(Free from your nearest Burpee branch): Warminster, PA 18974; Clinton, IA 52732; Riverside, CA 92502.
170 pages, 6 x 9. When seed catalogs are mentioned most people think "Burpee."

Grace's Gardens
100 Autumn Lane, Hackettstown, NJ 07840
16-page catalog of unusual seeds, "grow a complete 'believe it or not' food garden in less than ¼ acre." 25¢.

Johnny's Selected Seeds
Albion, ME 04910
28 pages, 5½ x 8½. Heirloom beans and corn; many hard-to-find seeds of Oriental vegetables. 25¢.

Kitazawa Seed Co.
356 W. Taylor St., San Jose, CA 95110
One-sheet listing of Oriental vegetables including bitter melon, Japanese pickling melon, *gobo*, and many varieties of more common Oriental vegetables.

Nichols Garden Nursery
1190 No. Pacific Highway, Albany, OR 97321
88 pages, 8½ x 11. Written by an enthusiastic gardener and cook who has searched the world for the unusual and rare in vegetables and herbs.

Geo. W. Park Seed Co., Inc.
Greenwood, SC 29646
122 pages, 8¼ x 11¼. A guide to quality and variety in flowers and vegetables. Includes indoor gardening. The most frequently "borrowed" seed catalog.

T. Sakata Seed Co.
120 Montgomery St., San Francisco, CA 94101

Tsang & Ma International
1556 Laurel St., San Carlos, CA 94070
One-page leaflet, 16 types of Chinese vegetables, including bitter melon and Chinese okra. $2 minimum order.

The young aromatic leaves of sansho are used as a garnish.